THINGS FALL APART

Chinua Achebe

This edition published by Spark Publishing

Spark Publishing
A Division of SparkNotes LLC
120 Fifth Avenue, 8th Floor
New York, NY 10011

Please submit all comments and questions or report errors to www.sparknotes.com/errors

Printed and bound in the United States

ISBN 1-58663-407-0

Introduction:
Stopping to Buy SparkNotes on a Snowy Evening

Whose words these are you *think* you know.
Your paper's due tomorrow, though;
We're glad to see you stopping here
To get some help before you go.

Lost your course? You'll find it here.
Face tests and essays without fear.
Between the words, good grades at stake:
Get great results throughout the year.

Once school bells caused your heart to quake
As teachers circled each mistake.
Use SparkNotes and no longer weep,
Ace every single test you take.

Yes, books are lovely, dark, and deep,
But only what you grasp you keep,
With hours to go before you sleep,
With hours to go before you sleep.

CONTENTS

CONTEXT   1

PLOT OVERVIEW   3

CHARACTER LIST   6

ANALYSIS OF MAJOR CHARACTERS   11
    OKONKWO   11
    NWOYE   12
    EZINMA   12
    MR. BROWN   12

THEMES, MOTIFS & SYMBOLS   14
    THE STRUGGLE BETWEEN CHANGE AND TRADITION   14
    VARYING INTERPRETATIONS OF MASCULINITY   15
    LANGUAGE AS A SIGN OF CULTURAL DIFFERENCE   15
    CHI   16
    ANIMAL IMAGERY   16
    LOCUSTS   17
    FIRE   17

SUMMARY & ANALYSIS   19
    CHAPTERS ONE–THREE   19
    CHAPTERS FOUR–SIX   22
    CHAPTERS SEVEN–EIGHT   25
    CHAPTERS NINE–ELEVEN   28
    CHAPTERS TWELVE–THIRTEEN   31
    CHAPTERS FOURTEEN–SIXTEEN   33
    CHAPTERS SEVENTEEN–NINETEEN   36
    CHAPTERS TWENTY–TWENTY-ONE   39
    CHAPTERS TWENTY-TWO–TWENTY-THREE   42
    CHAPTERS TWENTY-FOUR–TWENTY-FIVE   45

IMPORTANT QUOTATIONS EXPLAINED   49

KEY FACTS   53

STUDY QUESTIONS & ESSAY TOPICS   56
   STUDY QUESTIONS   56
   SUGGESTED ESSAY TOPICS   58

REVIEW & RESOURCES   59
   QUIZ   59
   SUGGESTIONS FOR FURTHER READING   64

CONTEXT

ALBERT CHINUALUMOGU ACHEBE WAS BORN ON November 16, 1930, in Ogidi, a large village in Nigeria. Although he was the child of a Protestant missionary and received his early education in English, his upbringing was multicultural, as the inhabitants of Ogidi still lived according to many aspects of traditional Igbo (formerly written as Ibo) culture. Achebe attended the Government College in Umuahia from 1944 to 1947. He graduated from University College, Ibadan, in 1953. While he was in college, Achebe studied history and theology. He also developed his interest in indigenous Nigerian cultures, and he rejected his Christian name, Albert, for his indigenous one, Chinua.

In the 1950s, Achebe was one of the founders of a Nigerian literary movement that drew upon the traditional oral culture of its indigenous peoples. In 1959, he published *Things Fall Apart* as a response to novels, such as Joseph Conrad's *Heart of Darkness,* that treat Africa as a primordial and cultureless foil for Europe. Tired of reading white men's accounts of how primitive, socially backward, and, most important, language-less native Africans were, Achebe sought to convey a fuller understanding of one African culture and, in so doing, give voice to an underrepresented and exploited colonial subject.

Things Fall Apart is set in the 1890s and portrays the clash between Nigeria's white colonial government and the traditional culture of the indigenous Igbo people. Achebe's novel shatters the stereotypical European portraits of native Africans. He is careful to portray the complex, advanced social institutions and artistic traditions of Igbo culture prior to its contact with Europeans. Yet he is just as careful not to stereotype the Europeans; he offers varying depictions of the white man, such as the mostly benevolent Mr. Brown, the zealous Reverend Smith, and the ruthlessly calculating District Commissioner.

Achebe's education in English and exposure to European customs have allowed him to capture both the European and the African perspectives on colonial expansion, religion, race, and culture. His decision to write *Things Fall Apart* in English is an important one. Achebe wanted this novel to respond to earlier colonial accounts of Africa; his choice of language was thus political. Unlike some later African authors who chose to revitalize native languages as a form of resistance to colonial culture, Achebe wanted to achieve cultural revitalization within and through English. Nevertheless, he manages to capture the rhythm of the Igbo language and he integrates Igbo vocabulary into the narrative.

Achebe has become renowned throughout the world as a father of modern African literature, essayist, and professor of English literature at Bard College in New York. But Achebe's achievements are most concretely reflected by his prominence in Nigeria's academic culture and in its literary and political institutions. He worked for the Nigerian Broadcasting Company for over a decade and later became an English professor at the University of Nigeria. He has also been quite influential in the publication of new Nigerian writers. In 1967, he co-founded a publishing company with a Nigerian poet named Christopher Okigbo and in 1971, he began editing *Okike,* a respected journal of Nigerian writing. In 1984, he founded *Uwa ndi Igbo,* a bilingual magazine containing a great deal of information about Igbo culture. He has been active in Nigerian politics since the 1960s, and many of his novels address the post-colonial social and political problems that Nigeria still faces.

Plot Overview

O KONKWO IS A WEALTHY AND RESPECTED WARRIOR of the Umuofia clan, a lower Nigerian tribe that is part of a consortium of nine connected villages. He is haunted by the actions of Unoka, his cowardly and spendthrift father, who died in disrepute, leaving many village debts unsettled. In response, Okonkwo becomes a clansman, warrior, farmer, and family provider extraordinaire. He has a twelve-year-old son named Nwoye whom he finds lazy; Okonkwo worries that Nwoye will end up a failure like Unoka.

In a settlement with a neighboring tribe, Umuofia wins a virgin and a fifteen-year-old boy. Okonkwo takes charge of the boy, Ikemefuna, and finds an ideal son in him. Nwoye likewise forms a strong attachment to the newcomer. Despite his fondness for Ikemefuna and despite the fact that the boy begins to call him "father," Okonkwo does not let himself show any affection for him.

During the Week of Peace, Okonkwo accuses his youngest wife, Ojiugo, of negligence. He severely beats her, breaking the peace of the sacred week. He makes some sacrifices to show his repentance, but he has shocked his community irreparably.

Ikemefuna stays with Okonkwo's family for three years. Nwoye looks up to him as an older brother and, much to Okonkwo's pleasure, develops a more masculine attitude. One day, the locusts come to Umuofia—they will come every year for seven years before disappearing for another generation. The village excitedly collects them because they are good to eat when cooked.

Ogbuefi Ezeudu, a respected village elder, informs Okonkwo in private that the Oracle has said that Ikemefuna must be killed. He tells Okonkwo that because Ikemefuna calls him "father," Okonkwo should not take part in the boy's death. Okonkwo lies to Ikemefuna, telling him that they must return him to his home village. Nwoye bursts into tears.

As he walks with the men of Umuofia, Ikemefuna thinks about seeing his mother. After several hours of walking, some of Okonkwo's clansmen attack the boy with machetes. Ikemefuna runs to Okonkwo for help. But Okonkwo, who doesn't wish to look weak in front of his fellow tribesmen, cuts the boy down despite the Oracle's admonishment. When Okonkwo returns home, Nwoye deduces that his friend is dead.

3

Okonkwo sinks into a depression, able neither to sleep nor eat. He visits his friend Obierika and begins to feel revived a bit. Okonkwo's daughter Ezinma falls ill, but she recovers after Okonkwo gathers leaves for her medicine.

The death of Ogbuefi Ezeudu is announced to the surrounding villages by means of the *ekwe,* a musical instrument. Okonkwo feels guilty because the last time Ezeudu visited him was to warn him against taking part in Ikemefuna's death. At Ogbuefi Ezeudu's large and elaborate funeral, the men beat drums and fire their guns. Tragedy compounds upon itself when Okonkwo's gun explodes and kills Ogbuefi Ezeudu's sixteen-year-old son.

Because killing a clansman is a crime against the earth goddess, Okonkwo must take his family into exile for seven years in order to atone. He gathers his most valuable belongings and takes his family to his mother's natal village, Mbanta. The men from Ogbuefi Ezeudu's quarter burn Okonkwo's buildings and kill his animals to cleanse the village of his sin.

Okonkwo's kinsmen, especially his uncle, Uchendu, receive him warmly. They help him build a new compound of huts and lend him yam seeds to start a farm. Although he is bitterly disappointed at his misfortune, Okonkwo reconciles himself to life in his motherland.

During the second year of Okonkwo's exile, Obierika brings several bags of cowries (shells used as currency) that he has made by selling Okonkwo's yams. Obierika plans to continue to do so until Okonkwo returns to the village. Obierika also brings the bad news that Abame, another village, has been destroyed by the white man.

Soon afterward, six missionaries travel to Mbanta. Through an interpreter named Mr. Kiaga, the missionaries' leader, Mr. Brown, speaks to the villagers. He tells them that their gods are false and that worshipping more than one God is idolatrous. But the villagers do not understand how the Holy Trinity can be accepted as one God. Although his aim is to convert the residents of Umuofia to Christianity, Mr. Brown does not allow his followers to antagonize the clan.

Mr. Brown grows ill and is soon replaced by Reverend James Smith, an intolerant and strict man. The more zealous converts are relieved to be free of Mr. Brown's policy of restraint. One such convert, Enoch, dares to unmask an *egwugwu* during the annual ceremony to honor the earth deity, an act equivalent to killing an ancestral spirit. The next day, the *egwugwu* burn Enoch's compound and Reverend Smith's church to the ground.

The District Commissioner is upset by the burning of the church and requests that the leaders of Umuofia meet with him. Once they are gathered, however, the leaders are handcuffed and thrown in jail, where they suffer insults and physical abuse.

After the prisoners are released, the clansmen hold a meeting, during which five court messengers approach and order the clansmen to desist. Expecting his fellow clan members to join him in uprising, Okonkwo kills their leader with his machete. When the crowd allows the other messengers to escape, Okonkwo realizes that his clan is not willing to go to war.

When the District Commissioner arrives at Okonkwo's compound, he finds that Okonkwo has hanged himself. Obierika and his friends lead the commissioner to the body. Obierika explains that suicide is a grave sin; thus, according to custom, none of Okonkwo's clansmen may touch his body. The commissioner, who is writing a book about Africa, believes that the story of Okonkwo's rebellion and death will make for an interesting paragraph or two. He has already chosen the book's title: *The Pacification of the Primitive Tribes of the Lower Niger.*

CHARACTER LIST

Okonkwo An influential clan leader in Umuofia. Since early childhood, Okonkwo's embarrassment about his lazy, squandering, and effeminate father, Unoka, has driven him to succeed. Okonkwo's hard work and prowess in war have earned him a position of high status in his clan, and he attains wealth sufficient to support three wives and their children. Okonkwo's tragic flaw is that he is terrified of looking weak like his father. As a result, he behaves rashly, bringing a great deal of trouble and sorrow upon himself and his family.

Nwoye Okonkwo's oldest son, who Okonkwo believes is weak and lazy. Okonkwo continually beats Nwoye, hoping to correct the faults that he perceives in him. Influenced by Ikemefuna, Nwoye begins to exhibit more masculine behavior, which pleases Okonkwo. He maintains, however, doubts about some of the laws and rules of his tribe and eventually converts to Christianity, an act that Okonkwo criticizes as "effeminate." Okonkwo believes that Nwoye is afflicted with the same weaknesses that his father, Unoka, possessed in abundance.

Ezinma The only child of Okonkwo's second wife, Ekwefi. As the only one of Ekwefi's ten children to survive past infancy, Ezinma is the center of her mother's world. Their relationship is atypical—Ezinma calls Ekwefi by her name and is treated by her as an equal. Ezinma is also Okonkwo's favorite child, for she understands him better than any of his other children and reminds him of Ekwefi when Ekwefi was the village beauty. Okonkwo rarely demonstrates his affection, however, because he fears that doing so would make him look weak. Furthermore, he wishes that Ezinma were a boy because she would have been the perfect son.

Ikemefuna A boy given to Okonkwo by a neighboring village. Ikemefuna lives in the hut of Okonkwo's first wife and quickly becomes popular with Okonkwo's children. He develops an especially close relationship with Nwoye, Okonkwo's oldest son, who looks up to him. Okonkwo too becomes very fond of Ikemefuna, who calls him "father" and is a perfect clansman, but Okonkwo does not demonstrate his affection because he fears that doing so would make him look weak.

Mr. Brown The first white missionary to travel to Umuofia. Mr. Brown institutes a policy of compromise, understanding, and non-aggression between his flock and the clan. He even becomes friends with prominent clansmen and builds a school and a hospital in Umuofia. Unlike Reverend Smith, he attempts to appeal respectfully to the tribe's value system rather than harshly impose his religion on it.

Reverend James Smith The missionary who replaces Mr. Brown. Unlike Mr. Brown, Reverend Smith is uncompromising and strict. He demands that his converts reject all of their indigenous beliefs, and he shows no respect for indigenous customs or culture. He is the stereotypical white colonialist, and his behavior epitomizes the problems of colonialism. He intentionally provokes his congregation, inciting it to anger and even indirectly, through Enoch, encouraging some fairly serious transgressions.

Uchendu   The younger brother of Okonkwo's mother. Uchendu receives Okonkwo and his family warmly when they travel to Mbanta and he advises Okonkwo to be grateful for the comfort that his motherland offers him lest he anger the dead—especially his mother, who is buried there. Uchendu himself has suffered—all but one of his six wives are dead and he has buried twenty-two children. He is a peaceful, compromising man and functions as a foil (a character whose emotions or actions highlight, by means of contrast, the emotions or actions of another character) to Okonkwo, who acts impetuously and without thinking.

The District Commissioner   An authority figure in the white colonial government in Nigeria. The prototypical racist colonialist, the District Commissioner thinks that he understands everything about native African customs and cultures and he has no respect for them. He plans to work his experiences into an ethnographic study on local African tribes, the idea of which embodies his dehumanizing and reductive attitude toward race relations.

Unoka   Okonkwo's father, of whom Okonkwo has been ashamed since childhood. By the standards of the clan, Unoka was a coward and a spendthrift. He never took a title in his life, he borrowed money from his clansmen, and he rarely repaid his debts. He never became a warrior because he feared the sight of blood. Moreover, he died of an abominable illness. On the positive side, Unoka appears to have been a talented musician and gentle, if idle. He may well have been a dreamer, ill suited to the chauvinistic culture into which he was born. The novel opens ten years after his death.

Obierika   Okonkwo's close friend, whose daughter's wedding provides cause for festivity early in the novel. Obierika looks out for his friend, selling Okonkwo's yams to ensure that Okonkwo won't suffer financial ruin while in exile and comforting Okonkwo when he is depressed. Like Nwoye, Obierika questions some of the tribe's traditional strictures.

Ekwefi   Okonkwo's second wife, once the village beauty. Ekwefi ran away from her first husband to live with Okonkwo. Ezinma is her only surviving child, her other nine having died in infancy, and Ekwefi constantly fears that she will lose Ezinma as well. Ekwefi is good friends with Chielo, the priestess of the goddess Agbala.

Enoch   A fanatical convert to the Christian church in Umuofia. Enoch's disrespectful act of ripping the mask off an egwugwu during an annual ceremony to honor the earth deity leads to the climactic clash between the indigenous and colonial justice systems. While Mr. Brown, early on, keeps Enoch in check in the interest of community harmony, Reverend Smith approves of his zealotry.

Ogbuefi Ezeudu   The oldest man in the village and one of the most important clan elders and leaders. Ogbuefi Ezeudu was a great warrior in his youth and now delivers messages from the Oracle.

Chielo   A priestess in Umuofia who is dedicated to the Oracle of the goddess Agbala. Chielo is a widow with two children. She is good friends with Ekwefi and is fond of Ezinma, whom she calls "my daughter." At one point, she carries Ezinma on her back for miles in order to help purify her and appease the gods.

Akunna   A clan leader of Umuofia. Akunna and Mr. Brown discuss their religious beliefs peacefully, and Akunna's influence on the missionary advances Mr. Brown's strategy for converting the largest number of clansmen by working with, rather than against, their belief system. In so doing, however, Akunna formulates an articulate and rational defense of his religious system and draws some striking parallels between his style of worship and that of the Christian missionaries.

Nwakibie   A wealthy clansmen who takes a chance on Okonkwo by lending him 800 seed yams—twice the number for which Okonkwo asks. Nwakibie thereby helps Okonkwo build up the beginnings of his personal wealth, status, and independence.

Mr. Kiaga   The native-turned-Christian missionary who arrives in Mbanta and converts Nwoye and many others.

Okagbue Uyanwa   A famous medicine man whom Okonkwo summons for help in dealing with Ezinma's health problems.

Maduka   Obierika's son. Maduka wins a wrestling contest in his mid-teens. Okonkwo wishes he had promising, manly sons like Maduka.

Obiageli   The daughter of Okonkwo's first wife. Although Obiageli is close to Ezinma in age, Ezinma has a great deal of influence over her.

Ojiugo   Okonkwo's third and youngest wife, and the mother of Nkechi. Okonkwo beats Ojiugo during the Week of Peace.

Analysis of Major Characters

Okonkwo

Okonkwo, the son of the effeminate and lazy Unoka, strives to make his way in a world that seems to value manliness. In so doing, he rejects everything for which he believes his father stood. Unoka was idle, poor, profligate, cowardly, gentle, and interested in music and conversation. Okonkwo consciously adopts opposite ideals and becomes productive, wealthy, thrifty, brave, violent, and adamantly opposed to music and anything else that he perceives to be "soft," such as conversation and emotion. He is stoic to a fault.

Okonkwo achieves great social and financial success by embracing these ideals. He marries three wives and fathers several children. Nevertheless, just as his father was at odds with the values of the community around him, so too does Okonkwo find himself unable to adapt to changing times as the white man comes to live among the Umuofians. As it becomes evident that compliance rather than violence constitutes the wisest principle for survival, Okonkwo realizes that he has become a relic, no longer able to function within his changing society.

Okonkwo is a tragic hero in the classical sense: although he is a superior character, his tragic flaw—the equation of manliness with rashness, anger, and violence—brings about his own destruction. Okonkwo is gruff, at times, and usually unable to express his feelings (the narrator frequently uses the word "inwardly" in reference to Okonkwo's emotions). But his emotions are indeed quite complex, as his "manly" values conflict with his "unmanly" ones, such as fondness for Ikemefuna and Ezinma. The narrator privileges us with information that Okonkwo's fellow clan members do not have—that Okonkwo surreptitiously follows Ekwefi into the forest in pursuit of Ezinma, for example—and thus allows us to see the tender, worried father beneath the seemingly indifferent exterior.

NWOYE

Nwoye, Okonkwo's oldest son, struggles in the shadow of his powerful, successful, and demanding father. His interests are different from Okonkwo's and resemble more closely those of Unoka, his grandfather. He undergoes many beatings, at a loss for how to please his father, until the arrival of Ikemefuna, who becomes like an older brother and teaches him a gentler form of successful masculinity. As a result, Okonkwo backs off, and Nwoye even starts to win his grudging approval. Nwoye remains conflicted, however: though he makes a show of scorning feminine things in order to please his father, he misses his mother's stories.

With the unconscionable murder of Ikemefuna, however, Nwoye retreats into himself and finds himself forever changed. His reluctance to accept Okonkwo's masculine values turns into pure embitterment toward him and his ways. When missionaries come to Mbanta, Nwoye's hope and faith are reawakened, and he eventually joins forces with them. Although Okonkwo curses his lot for having borne so "effeminate" a son and disowns Nwoye, Nwoye appears to have found peace at last in leaving the oppressive atmosphere of his father's tyranny.

EZINMA

Ezinma, Okonkwo's favorite daughter and the only child of Ekwefi, is bold in the way that she approaches—and even sometimes contradicts—her father. Okonkwo remarks to himself multiple times that he wishes she had been born a boy, since he considers her to have such a masculine spirit. Ezinma alone seems to win Okonkwo's full attention, affection, and, ironically, respect. She and he are kindred spirits, which boosts her confidence and precociousness. She grows into a beautiful young woman who sensibly agrees to put off marriage until her family returns from exile so as to help her father leverage his sociopolitical power most effectively. In doing so, she shows an approach similar to that of Okonkwo: she puts strategy ahead of emotion.

MR. BROWN

Mr. Brown represents Achebe's attempt to craft a well-rounded portrait of the colonial presence by tempering bad personalities with good ones. Mr. Brown's successor, Reverend Smith, is zealous, vengeful, small-minded, and manipulative; he thus stands in contrast to Mr. Brown, who, on the other hand, is benevolent if not always beneficent. Mr. Brown succeeds in winning a large number of converts because he listens to the villagers' stories, beliefs, and opinions. He also accepts the converts unconditionally. His conversation with Akunna represents this sympathetic stance. The derisive comments that Reverend Smith makes about Mr. Brown after the latter's departure illustrate the colonial intolerance for any kind of sympathy for, and genuine interest in, the native culture. The surname Brown hints at his ability to navigate successfully the clear-cut racial division between the colonizers and the colonized.

Themes, Motifs & Symbols

Themes

Themes are the fundamental and often universal ideas explored in a literary work.

The Struggle between Change and Tradition

As a story about a culture on the verge of change, *Things Fall Apart* deals with how the prospect and reality of change affect various characters. The tension about whether change should be privileged over tradition often involves questions of personal status. Okonkwo, for example, resists the new political and religious orders because he feels that they are not manly and that he himself will not be manly if he consents to join or even tolerate them. To some extent, Okonkwo's resistance of cultural change is also due to his fear of losing societal status. His sense of self-worth is dependent upon the traditional standards by which society judges him. This system of evaluating the self inspires many of the clan's outcasts to embrace Christianity. Long scorned, these outcasts find in the Christian value system a refuge from the Igbo cultural values that place them below everyone else. In their new community, these converts enjoy a more elevated status.

The villagers in general are caught between resisting and embracing change and they face the dilemma of trying to determine how best to adapt to the reality of change. Many of the villagers are excited about the new opportunities and techniques that the missionaries bring. This European influence, however, threatens to extinguish the need for the mastery of traditional methods of farming, harvesting, building, and cooking. These traditional methods, once crucial for survival, are now, to varying degrees, dispensable. Throughout the novel, Achebe shows how dependent such traditions are upon storytelling and language and thus how quickly the abandonment of the Igbo language for English could lead to the eradication of these traditions.

VARYING INTERPRETATIONS OF MASCULINITY

Okonkwo's relationship with his late father shapes much of his violent and ambitious demeanor. He wants to rise above his father's legacy of spendthrift, indolent behavior, which he views as weak and therefore feminine. This association is inherent in the clan's language—the narrator mentions that the word for a man who has not taken any of the expensive, prestige-indicating titles is *agbala,* which also means "woman." But, for the most part, Okonkwo's idea of manliness is not the clan's. He associates masculinity with aggression and feels that anger is the only emotion that he should display. For this reason, he frequently beats his wives, even threatening to kill them from time to time. We are told that he does not think about things, and we see him acting rashly and impetuously. Yet others who are in no way effeminate do not behave in this way. Obierika, unlike Okonkwo, "was a man who thought about things." Whereas Obierika refuses to accompany the men on the trip to kill Ikemefuna, Okonkwo not only volunteers to join the party that will execute his surrogate son but also violently stabs him with his machete simply because he is afraid of appearing weak.

Okonkwo's seven-year exile from his village only reinforces his notion that men are stronger than women. While in exile, he lives among the kinsmen of his motherland but resents the period in its entirety. The exile is his opportunity to get in touch with his feminine side and to acknowledge his maternal ancestors, but he keeps reminding himself that his maternal kinsmen are not as warlike and fierce as he remembers the villagers of Umuofia to be. He faults them for their preference of negotiation, compliance, and avoidance over anger and bloodshed. In Okonkwo's understanding, his uncle Uchendu exemplifies this pacifist (and therefore somewhat effeminate) mode.

LANGUAGE AS A SIGN OF CULTURAL DIFFERENCE

Language is an important theme in *Things Fall Apart* on several levels. In demonstrating the imaginative, often formal language of the Igbo, Achebe emphasizes that Africa is not the silent or incomprehensible country that books such as *Heart of Darkness* made it out to be. Rather, by peppering the novel with Igbo words, Achebe shows that the Igbo language is too complex for direct translation into English. Similarly, Igbo culture cannot be understood within the framework of European colonialist values. Achebe also points out that Africa has many *different* languages: the villagers of Umuofia, for example, make fun of Mr. Brown's translator because his language is slightly different from their own.

On a macroscopic level, it is extremely significant that Achebe chose to write *Things Fall Apart* in English—he clearly intended it to be read by the West at least as much, if not more, than by his fellow Nigerians. His goal was to critique and emend the portrait of Africa that was painted by so many writers of the colonial period. Doing so required the use of English, the language of those colonial writers. Through his inclusion of proverbs, folktales, and songs translated from the Igbo language, Achebe managed to capture and convey the rhythms, structures, cadences, and beauty of the Igbo language.

MOTIFS

Motifs are recurring structures, contrasts, or literary devices that can help to develop and inform the text's major themes.

CHI

The concept of *chi* is discussed at various points throughout the novel and is important to our understanding of Okonkwo as a tragic hero. The *chi* is an individual's personal god, whose merit is determined by the individual's good fortune or lack thereof. Along the lines of this interpretation, one can explain Okonkwo's tragic fate as the result of a problematic *chi*—a thought that occurs to Okonkwo at several points in the novel. For the clan believes, as the narrator tells us in Chapter Fourteen, a "man could not rise beyond the destiny of his *chi.*" But there is another understanding of *chi* that conflicts with this definition. In Chapter Four, the narrator relates, according to an Igbo proverb, that "when a man says yes his *chi* says yes also." According to this understanding, individuals will their own destinies. Thus, depending upon our interpretation of *chi*, Okonkwo seems either more or less responsible for his own tragic death. Okonkwo himself shifts between these poles: when things are going well for him, he perceives himself as master and maker of his own destiny; when things go badly, however, he automatically disavows responsibility and asks why he should be so ill fated.

ANIMAL IMAGERY

In their descriptions, categorizations, and explanations of human behavior and wisdom, the Igbo often use animal anecdotes to naturalize their rituals and beliefs. The presence of animals in their folklore reflects the environment in which they live—not yet "modernized" by European influence. Though the colonizers, for the most part, view the Igbo's understanding of the world as rudimentary, the Igbo perceive these animal stories, such as the account of how the tortoise's shell came to be bumpy, as logical explanations of natural phenomena. Another important animal image is the figure of the sacred python. Enoch's alleged killing and eating of the python symbolizes the transition to a new form of spirituality and a new religious order. Enoch's disrespect of the python clashes with the Igbo's reverence for it, epitomizing the incompatibility of colonialist and indigenous values.

SYMBOLS

Symbols are objects, characters, figures, or colors used to represent abstract ideas or concepts.

LOCUSTS

Achebe depicts the locusts that descend upon the village in highly allegorical terms that prefigure the arrival of the white settlers, who will feast on and exploit the resources of the Igbo. The fact that the Igbo eat these locusts highlights how innocuous they take them to be. Similarly, those who convert to Christianity fail to realize the damage that the culture of the colonizer does to the culture of the colonized.

The language that Achebe uses to describe the locusts indicates their symbolic status. The repetition of words like "settled" and "every" emphasizes the suddenly ubiquitous presence of these insects and hints at the way in which the arrival of the white settlers takes the Igbo off guard. Furthermore, the locusts are so heavy they break the tree branches, which symbolizes the fracturing of Igbo traditions and culture under the onslaught of colonialism and white settlement. Perhaps the most explicit clue that the locusts symbolize the colonists is Obierika's comment in Chapter Fifteen: "the Oracle . . . said that other white men were on their way. They were locusts. . . ."

FIRE

Okonkwo is associated with burning, fire, and flame throughout the novel, alluding to his intense and dangerous anger—the only emotion that he allows himself to display. Yet the problem with fire, as Okonkwo acknowledges in Chapters Seventeen and Twenty-Four, is that it destroys everything it consumes. Okonkwo is both physically destructive—he kills Ikemefuna and Ogbuefi Ezeudu's son—and emotionally destructive—he suppresses his fondness for Ikemefuna and Ezinma in favor of a colder, more masculine aura. Just as fire feeds on itself until all that is left is a pile of ash, Okonkwo eventually succumbs to his intense rage, allowing it to rule his actions until it destroys him.

Summary & Analysis

Chapters One–Three

> Turning and turning in the widening gyre
> The falcon cannot hear the falconer;
> Things fall apart; the center cannot hold;
> Mere anarchy is loosed upon the world.
> — W. B. Yeats, "The Second Coming"
> (See Quotations, p. 49)

Summary: Chapter One

> Among the Igbo . . . proverbs are the palm-oil with
> which words are eaten.
> (See Quotations, p. 50)

Okonkwo is a wealthy and respected warrior of the Umuofia clan, a lower Nigerian tribe that is part of a consortium of nine connected villages, including Okonkwo's village, Iguedo. In his youth, he brought honor to his village by beating Amalinze the Cat in a wrestling contest. Until his match with Okonkwo, the Cat had been undefeated for seven years. Okonkwo is completely unlike his now deceased father, Unoka, who feared the sight of blood and was always borrowing and losing money, which meant that his wife and children often went hungry. Unoka was, however, a skilled flute player and had a gift for, and love of, language.

Summary: Chapter Two

One night, the town crier rings the *ogene*, or gong, and requests that all of the clansmen gather in the market in the morning. At the gathering, Ogbuefi Ezeugo, a noted orator, announces that someone from the village of Mbaino murdered the wife of an Umuofia tribesman while she was in their market. The crowd expresses anger and indignation, and Okonkwo travels to Mbaino to deliver the message that they must hand over to Umuofia a virgin and a young man. Should Mbaino refuse to do so, the two villages must go to war, and Umuofia has a fierce reputation for its skill in war and magic. Okonkwo is chosen to represent his clan because he is its fiercest warrior. Earlier in the chapter, as he remembers his past victories, we learn about the five human heads that he has taken in battle. On important occasions, he drinks palm-wine from the first head that he captured. Not surprisingly, Mbaino agrees to Umuofia's terms. The elders give the virgin to Ogbuefi Udo as his wife but are not sure what to do with the fifteen-year-old boy, Ikemefuna. The elders decide to turn him over to Okonkwo for safekeeping and instruction. Okonkwo, in turn, instructs his first wife to care for Ikemefuna.

In addition to being a skilled warrior, Okonkwo is quite wealthy. He supports three wives and eight children, and each wife has her own hut. Okonkwo also has a barn full of yams, a shrine for his ancestors, and his own hut, called an *obi*.

Okonkwo fears weakness, a trait that he associates with his father and with women. When Okonkwo was a child, another boy called Unoka *agbala*, which is used to refer to women as well as to men who have not taken a title. Because he dreads weakness, Okonkwo is extremely demanding of his family. He finds his twelve-year-old son, Nwoye, to be lazy, so he beats and nags the boy constantly.

Summary: Chapter Three

Okonkwo built his fortune alone as a sharecropper because Unoka was never able to have a successful harvest. When he visited the Oracle, Unoka was told that he failed because of his laziness. Ill-fated, Unoka died of a shameful illness: "the swelling which was an abomination to the earth goddess." Those suffering from swelling stomachs and limbs are left in the Evil Forest to die so that they do not offend the earth by being buried. Unoka never held any of the community's four prestigious titles (because they must be paid for), and he left numerous debts unpaid.

As a result, Okonkwo cannot count on Unoka's help in building his own wealth and in constructing his *obi*. What's more, he has to work hard to make up for his father's negative strikes against him. Okonkwo succeeds in exceeding all the other clansmen as a warrior, a farmer, and a family provider. He begins by asking a wealthy clansman, Nwakibie, to give him 400 seed-yams to start a farm. Because Nwakibie admired Okonkwo's hard-working nature, he gave him eight hundred. One of Unoka's friends gave him another four hundred, but because of horrible droughts and relentless downpours, Okonkwo could keep only one third of the harvest. Some farmers who were lazier than Okonkwo put off planting their yams and thus avoided the grave losses suffered by Okonkwo and the other industrious farmers. That year's devastating harvest left a profound mark on Okonkwo, and for the rest of his life he considers his survival during that difficult period proof of his fortitude and inner mettle. Although his father tried to offer some words of comfort, Okonkwo felt only disgust for someone who would turn to words at a time when either actions or silence were called for.

ANALYSIS: CHAPTERS ONE–THREE

We are introduced immediately to the complex laws and customs of Okonkwo's clan and its commitment to harmonious relations. For example, the practice of sharing palm-wine and kola nuts is repeated throughout the book to emphasize the peacefulness of the Igbo. When Unoka's resentful neighbor visits him to collect a debt, the neighbor does not immediately address the debt. Instead, he and Unoka share a kola nut and pray to their ancestral spirits; afterward, they converse about community affairs at great length. The customs regulating social relations emphasize their common interests and culture, diffusing possible tension. The neighbor further eases the situation by introducing the subject of debt through a series of Igbo proverbs, thus making use of a shared oral tradition, as Okonkwo does when he asks Nwakibie for some seed-yams. Through his emphasis on the harmony and complexity of the Igbo, Achebe contradicts the stereotypical, European representations of Africans as savages.

Another important way in which Achebe challenges such stereotypical representations is through his use of language. As Achebe writes in his essay on Joseph Conrad's novella *Heart of Darkness,* colonialist Europe tended to perceive Africa as a foil or negation of Western culture and values, imagining Africa to be a primordial land of silence. But the people of Umuofia speak a complex language full of proverbs and literary and rhetorical devices. Achebe's translation of the Igbo language into English retains the cadences, rhythms, and speech patterns of the language without making them sound, as Conrad did, "primitive."

Okonkwo is the protagonist of *Things Fall Apart,* and, in addition to situating him within his society, the first few chapters of the novel offer us an understanding of his nature. He is driven by his hatred of his father, Unoka, and his fear of becoming like him. To avoid picking up Unoka's traits, Okonkwo acts violently without thinking, often provoking avoidable fights. He has a bad temper and rules his household with fear. Okonkwo associates Unoka with weakness, and with weakness he associates femininity. Because his behavior is so markedly different from his father's, he believes that it constitutes masculinity. However, it strains his relationship with Nwoye and leads him to sin in Chapter Four by breaking the Week of Peace. His rash behavior also causes tension within the community because he expresses disdain for less successful men. Ikemefuna later demonstrates that masculinity need not preclude kindness, gentleness, and affection, and Nwoye responds far more positively to Ikemefuna's nurturing influence than to Okonkwo's heavy-handedness.

Despite its focus on kinship, the Igbo social structure offers a greater chance for mobility than that of the colonizers who eventually arrive in Umuofia. Though ancestors are revered, a man's worth is determined by his own actions. In contrast to much of continental European society during the nineteenth century, which was marked by wealth-based class divisions, Igbo culture values individual displays of prowess, as evidenced by their wrestling competitions. Okonkwo is thus able, by means of his own efforts, to attain a position of wealth and prestige, even though his father died, penniless and titleless, of a shameful illness.

CHAPTERS FOUR–SIX

SUMMARY: CHAPTER FOUR

The clan decides that Ikemefuna will stay with Okonkwo. Ikemefuna is homesick and scared at first, but Nwoye's mother treats him as one of her own, and he is immediately popular with Okonkwo's children. Ikemefuna knows many stories that the children have never heard before and he possesses many impressive skills, such as making flutes out of bamboo sticks and setting traps for little bush rodents. To Okonkwo's delight, he also becomes like an older brother to Nwoye. Okonkwo himself grows quite fond of Ikemefuna, but he does not show any affection because he considers doing so a sign of weakness, which he refuses to tolerate in himself or others. Ikemefuna soon begins to call Okonkwo "father."

During the Week of Peace, Okonkwo notices that his youngest wife, Ojiugo, has left her hut to have her hair braided without having cooked dinner. He beats her for her negligence, shamefully breaking the peace of the sacred week in a transgression known as *nso-ani*. The priest demands that Okonkwo sacrifice a nanny goat and a hen and pay a fine of one length of cloth and one hundred cowries (shells used as currency). Okonkwo truly repents for his sin and follows the priest's orders. Ogbuefi Ezeudu observes that the punishment for breaking the Peace of Ani has become mild in Umuofia. He also criticizes another clan's practice of throwing the bodies of all who die during the Week of Peace into the Evil Forest.

After the Week of Peace, the villagers begin to clear the land in preparation for planting their farms. Nwoye and Ikemefuna help Okonkwo prepare the seed-yams, but he finds fault with their work. Even though he knows that they are too young to understand farming completely, he hopes that criticism will drive his son to be a great man and farmer. Ikemefuna settles into Okonkwo's family and shares his large stock of folk tales.

Summary: Chapter Five

Just before the harvest, the village holds the Feast of the New Yam to give thanks to the earth goddess, Ani. Okonkwo doesn't really care for feasts because he considers them times of idleness. The women thoroughly scrub and decorate their huts, throw away all of their unused yams from the previous year, and use cam wood to paint their skin and that of their children with decorative designs. With nothing to do, Okonkwo becomes angry, and he finally comes up with an excuse to beat his second wife, Ekwefi. He then decides to go hunting with his gun. Okonkwo is not a good hunter, however, and Ekwefi mutters a snide remark under her breath about "guns that never shot." In a fit of fury, he shoots the gun at her but misses.

The annual wrestling contest comes the day after the feast. Ekwefi, in particular, enjoys the contest because Okonkwo won her heart when he defeated the Cat. He was too poor to pay her bride-price then, but she later ran away from her husband to be with him. Ezinma, Ekwefi's only child, takes a bowl of food to Okonkwo's hut. Okonkwo is very fond of Ezinma but rarely demonstrates his affection. Obiageli, the daughter of Okonkwo's first wife, is already there, waiting for him to finish the meal that she has brought him. Nkechi, the daughter of Okonkwo's third wife, Ojiugo, then brings a meal to Okonkwo.

Summary: Chapter Six

The wrestling match takes place on the village *ilo,* or common green. Drummers line the field, and the spectators are so excited that they must be held back. The wrestling begins with matches between boys ages fifteen and sixteen. Maduka, the son of Okonkwo's friend Obierika, wins one match within seconds. As the wrestling continues, Ekwefi speaks with Chielo, the priestess of Agbala, the Oracle of the Hills and Caves. The two women are good friends, and Chielo inquires about Ezinma, whom she calls "my daughter." They conclude that Ezinma seems to have "come to stay" because she has reached the age of ten.

ANALYSIS: CHAPTERS FOUR–SIX

Whereas the first few chapters highlight the complexity and originality of the Igbo language, in these chapters Achebe points out another aspect of Igbo culture that colonialist Europe tended to ignore: the existence of subcultures within a given African population. Each clan has its own stories, and Ikemefuna is an exciting addition to Umuofia because he brings with him new and unfamiliar folk tales. With the introduction of Ikemefuna, Achebe is able to remind us that the story we are reading is not about Africa but rather about one specific culture within Africa. He thus combats the European tendency to see all Africans as one and the same.

The religious values of the Igbo emphasize the shared benefits of peaceful, harmonious relations. The Igbo always consult the Oracle before declaring war, for they fear punishment from their gods should they declare war without just cause. Their religion also emphasizes the individual's obligation to the community. When Okonkwo breaks the peace during the sacred week, the priest chastises him for endangering the entire community by risking the earth deity's wrath. He refuses Okonkwo's offer of a kola nut, expressing disagreement peacefully. This parrying of potential violence on the interpersonal level reflects the culture's tradition of avoiding violence and war whenever possible.

Moreover, the belief in the *chi,* an individual's personal god, also smooths possible tensions in the Igbo community. The *chi* allows individuals to attribute some portion of their failures and successes to divine influence, thus lessening the shame of the former and pride of the latter. This belief encourages respect between individuals; the men are thus able to settle a dispute between Okonkwo and a man whom he insults without resorting to personal attacks.

Although traditional Igbo culture is fairly democratic in nature, it is also profoundly patriarchal. Wife-beating is an accepted practice. Moreover, femininity is associated with weakness while masculinity is associated with strength. It is no coincidence that the word that refers to a titleless man also means "woman." A man is not believed to be "manly" if he cannot control his women. Okonkwo frequently beats his wives, and the only emotion he allows himself to display is anger. He does not particularly like feasts, because the idleness that they involve makes him feel emasculated. Okonkwo's frustration at this idleness causes him to act violently, breaking the spirit of the celebration.

Okonkwo's extremely overactive desire to conquer and subdue, along with his profound hatred of all things feminine, is suggestive of impotence. Though he has children, Okonkwo is never compared to anything thriving or organic; instead, Achebe always associates him with fire, which consumes but does not beget. The incident in which he tries to shoot Ekwefi with his gun is likewise suggestive of impotence. After Ekwefi hints at Okonkwo's inability to shoot properly, Okonkwo proves this inability, failing to hit Ekwefi. Impotence, whether or not it is an actual physical condition for him, seems to be a characteristic that is related to Okonkwo's chauvinistic behavior.

CHAPTERS SEVEN–EIGHT

SUMMARY: CHAPTER SEVEN

> *And at last the locusts did descend. They settled on*
> *every tree and on every blade of grass....*
> *(See* QUOTATIONS, *p. 50)*

Ikemefuna stays with Okonkwo's family for three years. He seems to have "kindled a new fire" in Nwoye, who, much to Okonkwo's pleasure, becomes more masculine in his attitude. Okonkwo knows that his son's development is a result of Ikemefuna's influence. He frequently invites the two into his *obi* to listen to violent, masculine stories. Although Nwoye misses his mother's stories, he knows that he pleases his father when he expresses disdain for women and their concerns.

To the village's surprise, locusts descend upon Umuofia. They come once in a generation and will return every year for seven years before disappearing for another lifetime. The village excitedly collects them because they are good to eat when cooked. Ogbuefi Ezeudu pays Okonkwo a visit, but he will not enter the hut to share the meal. Outside, he informs Okonkwo in private that the Oracle has decreed that Ikemefuna must be killed. He tells Okonkwo not to take part in the boy's death as Ikemefuna calls him "father." Okonkwo lies to Ikemefuna, telling him that he will be returning to his home village. Nwoye bursts into tears.

During the long walk home with the men of Umuofia, Ikemefuna thinks about seeing his mother. After hours of walking, a man attacks him with a machete. Ikemefuna cries to Okonkwo for help.

Okonkwo doesn't wish to look weak, so he cuts the boy down. When Okonkwo returns home, Nwoye intuits that his friend is dead. Something breaks inside him for the second time in his life; the first time was when he heard an infant crying in the Evil Forest, where newborn twins are left to die.

SUMMARY: CHAPTER EIGHT
Okonkwo sinks into a depression. He feels weak, and he cannot sleep or eat. When Ezinma brings him his evening meal three days later, she tells him that he must finish everything. He repeatedly wishes that she were a boy, and he berates himself for acting like a "shivering old woman." He visits his friend Obierika and congratulates Maduka on his successful wrestling. Obierika, in turn, requests that Okonkwo stay when his daughter's suitor arrives to determine a bride-price. Okonkwo complains to Obierika that his sons are not manly enough and says that he would be happier if Ezinma were a boy because she has "the right spirit." He and Obierika then argue over whether it was right of Okonkwo to partake in Ikemefuna's death.

Okonkwo begins to feel revived a bit. He decides that his unhappiness was a product of his idleness—if Ikemefuna had been murdered at a busier time of the year, he, Okonkwo, would have been completely undisturbed. Someone arrives to report the death of the oldest man in a neighboring village. Strangely, the old man's wife died shortly thereafter. Okonkwo questions the man's reputed strength once he learns how attached he had been to his wife.

Okonkwo sits with Obierika while Obierika bargains his daughter's bride-price with the family of her suitor. Afterward, Obierika and his future son-in-law's relatives talk about the differing customs in other villages. They discuss the practice of, and skill at, tapping palm trees for palm-wine. Obierika talks about hearing stories of men with skin as white as chalk. Another man, Machi, pipes in that such a man passes through the village frequently and that his name is Amadi. Those who know Amadi, a leper, laugh—the polite term for leprosy is "the white skin."

ANALYSIS: CHAPTERS SEVEN–EIGHT
Okonkwo disobeys the authority and advice of a clan elder in killing Ikemefuna. His actions are too close to killing a kinsman, which is a grave sin in Igbo culture. Okonkwo is so afraid of looking weak that he is willing to come close to violating tribal law in order to prove

otherwise. No one would have thought that Okonkwo was weak if he had stayed in the village. In fact, Obierika's opinion on the matter suggests that doing so would have been considered the more appropriate action. Instead, Okonkwo's actions seriously damage both his relationship with Nwoye and Nwoye's allegiance to Igbo society.

Nwoye shows promise because he voices chauvinist opinions, but his comments are really aimed at Okonkwo. In fact, Nwoye loves women's stories and is pleased when his mother or Okonkwo's other wives ask him to do things for them. He also seeks comfort in his mother's hut after Ikemefuna's death. Nwoye's questioning of Ikemefuna's death and of the practice of throwing away newborn twins is understandable: Obierika, too, frequently questions tradition. In fact, Obierika refused to accompany the other men to kill Ikemefuna, and Okonkwo points out that Obierika seems to question the Oracle. Obierika also has reservations about the village's practice of tapping trees. Okonkwo, on the other hand, accepts all of his clan's laws and traditions unquestioningly.

Interestingly, Obierika's manliness is never questioned. The fact that Obierika is skeptical of some Igbo practices makes us regard Nwoye's skepticism in a different light. We understand that, in Umuofia, manhood does not require the denigration of women. Like Nwoye, Ikemefuna is not close to his biological father. Rather, his primary emotional attachments to his natal village are to his mother and little sister.

Although he is not misogynistic like Okonkwo, Ikemefuna is the perfect clansman. He eagerly takes part in the community celebrations and integrates himself into Okonkwo's family. Okonkwo and Ikemefuna love one another as father and son, and Ikemefuna is a good older brother to Nwoye. Most important, he is protective rather than critical. He does not allow Nwoye and his brothers to tell their mother that Obiageli broke her water pot when she was showing off—he does not want her to be punished. Ikemefuna illustrates that manliness does not preclude gentleness and affection.

In calling himself a "shivering old woman," Okonkwo associates weakness with femininity. Although he denigrates his emotional attachment to Ikemefuna, he seeks comfort in his affectionate friendship with Obierika. Ezinma is likewise a source of great comfort to him. Because she understands him, she does not address his sorrow directly; rather, she urges him to eat. For all of Okonkwo's chauvinism, Ezinma is his favorite child. Okonkwo's frequently voiced desire that Ezinma were a boy seems to suggest that he secretly desires affectionate attachment with his actual sons, although he avoids admitting as much because he fears affection as a weakness. It is interesting to note that Okonkwo doesn't wish that Ezinma were a boy because she exhibits desirable masculine traits; rather, it is their bond of sympathy and understanding that he values.

CHAPTERS NINE–ELEVEN

SUMMARY: CHAPTER NINE
Ekwefi awakes Okonkwo very early in the morning and tells him that Ezinma is dying. Okonkwo ascertains that Ezinma has a fever and sets about collecting medicine. Ezinma is Ekwefi's only child and the "center of her world." Ekwefi is very lenient with her: Ezinma calls her by her first name and the dynamic of their relationship approaches equality.

Ekwefi's nine other children died in infancy. She developed the habit of naming them symbolic things such as "Onwumbiko," which means, "Death, I implore you," and "Ozoemena," which means, "May it not happen again." Okonkwo consulted a medicine man who told him that an *ogbanje* was tormenting them. An *ogbanje* is a "wicked" child that continually re-enters its mother's womb only to die again and again, causing its parents grief. A medicine man mutilated the dead body of Ekwefi's third child to discourage the *ogbanje*'s return. When Ezinma was born, like most *ogbanje* children, she suffered many illnesses, but she recovered from all of them. A year before the start of the novel, when Ezinma was nine, a medicine man named Okagbue Uyanwa found her *iyi-uwa*, the small, buried pebble that is the *ogbanje*'s physical link to the spirit world. Although the discovery of the *iyi-uwa* ought to have solved Ezinma's problems, every illness that Ezinma catches still brings terror and anxiety to Ekwefi.

SUMMARY: CHAPTER TEN
The village holds a ceremonial gathering to administer justice. The clan's ancestral spirits, which are known as *egwugwu*, emerge from a secret house into which no woman is allowed to step. The *egwugwu* take the form of masked men, and everyone suspects that Okonkwo is among them. The women and children are filled with fear even though they sense that the *egwugwu* are merely men impersonating spirits.

The first dispute that comes before the *egwugwu* involves an estranged husband and wife. The husband, Uzowulu, states that the three brothers of his wife, Mgbafo, beat him and took her and the children from his hut but would not return her bride-price. The woman's brothers state that he is a beastly man who beat their sister mercilessly, even causing her to miscarry once. They argue that Uzowulu must beg Mgbafo to return to him. If she agrees, the brothers declare, Uzowulu must understand that they will cut his genitals off if he ever beats her again. The *egwugwu* decide in favor of Mgbafo. One village elder complains that such a trifling matter should not be brought before them.

SUMMARY: CHAPTER ELEVEN

Ekwefi tells Ezinma a story about a greedy, cunning tortoise. All of the birds have been invited to a feast in the sky and Tortoise persuades the birds to lend him feathers to make wings so that he can attend the feast as well. As they travel to the feast, Tortoise also persuades them to take new names for the feast according to custom. He tells the birds that his name will be "All of you." When they arrive, Tortoise asks his hosts for whom the feast is prepared. They reply, "For all of you." Tortoise proceeds to eat and drink the best parts of the food and wine. The birds, angry and disgruntled at receiving only scraps, take back the feathers that they had given to Tortoise so that he is unable to fly home. Tortoise persuades Parrot to deliver a message to his wife: he wants her to cover their compound with their soft things so that he may jump from the sky without danger. Maliciously, Parrot tells Tortoise's wife to bring out all of the hard things. When Tortoise jumps, his shell breaks into pieces on impact. A medicine man puts it together again, which is why Tortoise's shell is not smooth.

Chielo, in her role as priestess, informs Ekwefi that Agbala, Oracle of the Hills and Caves, wishes to see Ezinma. Frightened, Okonkwo and Ekwefi try to persuade Chielo to wait until morning, but Chielo angrily reminds Okonkwo that he must not defy a god's will. Chielo takes Ezinma on her back and forbids anyone to follow. Ekwefi overcomes her fear of divine punishment and follows anyway. Chielo, carrying Ezinma, makes her rounds of the nine villages. When Chielo finally enters the Oracle's cave, Ekwefi resolves that if she hears Ezinma crying she will rush in to defend her—even against a god. Okonkwo startles her when he arrives at the cave with a machete. He calms Ekwefi and sits with her. She remembers when she ran away from her first husband to be Okonkwo's wife. When he answered her knock at his door, they exchanged no words. He led her to his bed and began to undo her clothing.

ANALYSIS: CHAPTERS NINE–ELEVEN

The relationship between Ekwefi and Ezinma is not a typical parent-child relationship; it is more like one between equals. Ekwefi receives a great deal of comfort and companionship from her daughter and, because she has lost so many children, she loves and respects her daughter all the more. Although motherhood is regarded as the crowning achievement of a woman's life, Ekwefi prizes Ezinma so highly not for the status motherhood brings her but rather for the love and companionship that she offers.

Mutually supportive interaction between women receives increasing focus as the novel progresses. For example, Okonkwo's wives frequently try to protect one another from his anger. Before Ezinma's birth, Ekwefi was not jealous of Okonkwo's first wife; she only expressed bitterness at her own misfortune. While Okonkwo gathers medicine for the fever, his other wives try to calm Ekwefi's fear. Ekwefi's friendship with Chielo, too, is an example of female bonding.

The incident with Chielo creates a real dilemma for Ekwefi, whose fear of the possible repercussions of disobeying her shows that Chielo's role as a priestess is taken seriously—it is not just ceremonial. But Ekwefi and Okonkwo's love for their child is strong enough that they are willing to defy religious authority. Although she has lost nine children, Ekwefi has been made strong by suffering, and when she follows Chielo, she chooses her daughter over the gods. In doing so, Ekwefi contradicts Okonkwo's ideas of femininity and demonstrates that strength and bravery are not only masculine attributes. Okonkwo also disobeys Chielo and follows her to the caves. But he, too, is careful to show respect to Chielo. She is a woman, but, as a priestess, she can order and chastise him openly. Her authority is not to be taken lightly.

Unlike the narration of Chielo's kidnapping of Ezinma, the narration of the *egwugwu* ceremony is rather ironic. The narrator makes several comments to reveal to us that the villagers know that the *egwugwu* are not real. For example, the narrator tells us: "Okonkwo's wives, and perhaps other women as well, might have noticed that the second *egwugwu* had the springy walk of Okonkwo. And they might have noticed that Okonkwo was not among the titled men and elders who sat . . . But if they thought these things they kept them within themselves." The narration of the incident of the medicine man and the *iyi-uwa* seems likewise to contain a trace of irony. After discussing the *iyi-uwa* and *egwugwu* in a tone that approaches mockery on a few occasions, the narrator, remarkably, says nothing that seems to undermine the villagers' perception of the strength of Chielo's divine power.

The story that Ekwefi tells Ezinma about Tortoise and the birds is one of the many instances in which we are exposed to Igbo folklore. The tale also seems to prepare us, like the symbolic locusts that arrive in Chapter Seven, for the colonialism that will soon descend upon Umuofia. Tortoise convinces the birds to allow him to come with them, even though he does not belong. He then appropriates all of their food. The tale presents two different ways of defeating Tortoise: first, the birds strip Tortoise of the feathers that they had lent him. This strategy involves cooperation and unity among the birds. When they refuse to concede to Tortoise's desires, Tortoise becomes unable to overpower them. Parrot's trick suggests a second course of action: by taking advantage of the position as translator, Parrot outwits Tortoise.

CHAPTERS TWELVE–THIRTEEN

SUMMARY: CHAPTER TWELVE

At dawn, Chielo exits the shrine with Ezinma on her back. Without saying a word, she takes Ezinma to Ekwefi's hut and puts her to bed. It turns out that Okonkwo was extremely worried the night before, although he did not show it. He forced himself to wait a while before walking to the Oracle's shrine. When he found it empty, he realized that Chielo was making her rounds to the nine villages, so he returned home to wait. In all, he made four trips to and from the caves. By the time he departed for the cave for the last time, Okonkwo was "gravely worried."

Okonkwo's family begins to prepare for Obierika's daughter's *uri*, a betrothal ceremony. The villagers contribute food to the festivities and Obierika buys a huge goat to present to his future in-laws. The preparations are briefly interrupted when the women retrieve an escaped cow and the cow's owner pays a fine for setting his cows loose on his neighbors' farms. The suitor's family members arrive and settle the clan's doubts about their generosity by bringing an impressive fifty pots of wine to the celebration. The women greet the visitors and the men exchange ceremonial greetings. The feast is a success.

SUMMARY: CHAPTER THIRTEEN

Ogbuefi Ezeudu's death is announced to the surrounding villages with the ekwe, a musical instrument. Okonkwo shudders. The last time Ezeudu visited him was to warn him against taking part in Ikemefuna's death. Since Ezeudu was a great warrior who took three of the clan's four titles, his funeral is large and elaborate. The men beat drums and fire their guns. Okonkwo's gun accidentally explodes and kills Ezeudu's sixteen-year-old son.

Killing a clansman is a crime against the earth goddess, so Okonkwo must atone by taking his family into exile for seven years. Okonkwo gathers his most valuable belongings and takes his family to his mother's natal village, Mbanta. According to the mandates of tradition, the men from Ezeudu's quarter burn Okonkwo's buildings and kill his animals to cleanse the village of his sin. Obierika questions why a man should suffer so much for an accidental killing. He then mourns the deaths of his wife's twins, whom he was forced to throw away, wondering what crime they committed.

ANALYSIS: CHAPTERS TWELVE–THIRTEEN

In the previous section, we see Okonkwo's behavior the night of the incident with Chielo as it appears to Ekwefi: Okonkwo shows up with his machete and fulfills the role of the strong, manly protector. At the beginning of Chapter Twelve, though, the narrator focuses on Okonkwo's internal state and we see his true feelings rather than his apparent ones. Because Okonkwo views affection as a sign of weakness, he forces himself to wait before following Chielo. Each time he makes the trip to the caves and finds her missing, he returns home again to wait. Not until his fourth trip does he encounter Ekwefi. Okonkwo is not the cruel, heartless man that he presents himself to be; rather, he is gravely worried about Ezinma's welfare. His hyperbolic understanding of manliness—the result of his tragic flaw—prevents his better nature from showing itself fully. Chielo's actions force Okonkwo to acknowledge how important his wife and child are to him.

The importance of kinship bonds in manifests itself in the ramifications of the violation of such bonds. When Ikemefuna enters Okonkwo's family as a surrogate son, he begins to heal the tension that exists between Okonkwo and Nwoye as a result of Okonkwo's difficulty in dealing with the memory of his father. Ikemefuna is thus presented as a possible solution to Okonkwo's tragic flaw. But Okonkwo fails to overcome his flaw and, in killing the boy who has become his son, damages his relationship with Nwoye permanently.

Moreover, he seriously injures Nwoye's respect for, and adherence to, Igbo cultural tradition.

Okonkwo's accidental killing of Ezeudu's son seems more than coincidence. We sense that it is a form of punishment for his earlier violation of kinship bonds. Just before the ill-fated incident happens, the one-handed spirit calls out to Ezeudu's corpse, "If your death was the death of nature, go in peace. But if a man caused it, do not allow him a moment's rest." Although the explosion of Okonkwo's gun moments later is not evidence that Okonkwo is, in fact, responsible for Ezeudu's death, it seems to suggest that Okonkwo's killing of Ikemefuna has been hurtful to the well-being and solidarity of the clan and its traditions.

Okonkwo's punishment emphasizes the importance of strong, harmonious relations within the community. Although Obierika questions the harsh punishment that Okonkwo receives for such an accident, the punishment, in a way, helps stave off anger, resentment, and, ultimately, revenge. Despite the accidental nature of the death of Ezeudu's son, it is understandable for Ezeudu's close relatives to be angry with Okonkwo. The burning of Okonkwo's compound displaces this anger onto his property, while Okonkwo's exile separates him temporarily from the offended community. Over a period of seven years, any remaining anger and resentment from Ezeudu's close relatives will dissipate, and the offender's place in the community will be restored.

CHAPTERS FOURTEEN–SIXTEEN

SUMMARY: CHAPTER FOURTEEN

Okonkwo's uncle, Uchendu, and the rest of his kinsmen receive him warmly. They help him build a new compound of huts and lend him yam seeds to start a farm. Soon, the rain that signals the beginning of the farming season arrives, in the unusual form of huge drops of hail. Okonkwo works hard on his new farm but with less enthusiasm than he had the first time around. He has toiled all his life because he wanted "to become one of the lords of the clan," but now that possibility is gone. Uchendu perceives Okonkwo's disappointment but waits to speak with him until after his son's wedding. Okonkwo takes part in the ceremony.

The following day, Uchendu gathers together his entire family, including Okonkwo. He points out that one of the most common names they give is Nneka, meaning "Mother is Supreme"—a man belongs to his fatherland and stays there when life is good, but he seeks refuge in his motherland when life is bitter and harsh. Uchendu uses the analogy of children, who belong to their fathers but seek refuge in their mothers' huts when their fathers beat them. Uchendu advises Okonkwo to receive the comfort of the motherland gratefully. He reminds Okonkwo that many have been worse off—Uchendu himself has lost all but one of his six wives and buried twenty-two children. Even so, Uchendu tells Okonkwo, "I did not hang myself, and I am still alive."

SUMMARY: CHAPTER FIFTEEN

During the second year of Okonkwo's exile, Obierika brings several bags of cowries to Okonkwo. He also brings bad news: a village named Abame has been destroyed. It seems that a white man arrived in Abame on an "iron horse" (which we find out later is a bicycle) during the planting season. The village elders consulted their oracle, which prophesied that the white man would be followed by others, who would bring destruction to Abame. The villagers killed the white man and tied his bicycle to their sacred tree to prevent it from getting away and telling the white man's friends. A while later, a group of white men discovered the bicycle and guessed their comrade's fate. Weeks later, a group of men surrounded Abame's market and destroyed almost everybody in the village. Uchendu asks Obierika what the first white man said to the villagers. Obierika replies that he said nothing, or rather, he said things that the villagers did not understand. Uchendu declares that Abame was foolish to kill a man who said nothing. Okonkwo agrees that the villagers were fools, but he believes that they should have heeded the oracle's warning and armed themselves.

The reason for Obierika's visit and for the bags of cowries that he brings Okonkwo is business. Obierika has been selling the biggest of Okonkwo's yams and also some of his seed-yams. He has given others to sharecroppers for planting. He plans to continue to bring Okonkwo the money from his yams until Okonkwo returns to Iguedo.

SUMMARY: CHAPTER SIXTEEN

Two years after his first visit (and three years after Okonkwo's exile), Obierika returns to Mbanta. He has decided to visit Okonkwo because he has seen Nwoye with some of the Christian missionaries who have arrived. Most of the other converts, Obierika finds, have been *efulefu,* men who hold no status and who are generally ignored by the clan. Okonkwo will not talk about Nwoye, but Nwoye's mother tells Obierika some of the story.

The narrator tells the story of Nwoye's conversion: six missionaries, headed by a white man, travel to Mbanta. The white man speaks to the village through an interpreter, who, we learn later, is named Mr. Kiaga. The interpreter's dialect incites mirthful laughter because he always uses Umuofia's word for "my buttocks" when he means "myself." He tells the villagers that they are all brothers and sons of God. He accuses them of worshipping false gods of wood and stone. The missionaries have come, he tells his audience, to persuade the villagers to leave their false gods and accept the one true God. The villagers, however, do not understand how the Holy Trinity can be accepted as one God. They also cannot see how God can have a son and not a wife. Many of them laugh and leave after the interpreter asserts that Umuofia's gods are incapable of doing any harm. The missionaries then burst into evangelical song. Okonkwo thinks that these newcomers must be insane, but Nwoye is instantly captivated. The "poetry of the new religion" seems to answer his questions about the deaths of Ikemefuna and the twin newborns, soothing him "like the drops of frozen rain melting on the dry palate."

ANALYSIS: CHAPTERS FOURTEEN–SIXTEEN

Okonkwo's exile forces him into his motherland. He doesn't deal well with his misfortune because he is so intent on being as successful and influential as his father was poor and powerless. His initial lack of gratitude toward his mother's kinsmen is a transgression of Igbo cultural values. His exile also upsets him because it forces him to spend time in a "womanly" place. He remains unwilling to admit to, or come to terms with, the feminine side of his personality.

Unoka's words regarding the bitterness of failing alone are important considering Okonkwo's present situation. Like Unoka, Uchendu reminds Okonkwo that he does not suffer alone. Uchendu laments the loss of five of his wives, openly expressing his strong attachment to the women who have shared his life and borne his children. He mentions that his remaining wife is a young girl who "does not know her left from her right." Youth, beauty, and sexual attractiveness are not the only things one should value in a wife, he argues. Uchendu also values wisdom, intelligence, and experience in a wife. Each and every death has caused him pain. Although we would not know it from Okonkwo, a father grieves for lost children just as a mother does.

The introduction of the European missionaries is not presented as a tragic event—it even contains some comical elements. The villagers, for example, mock the interpreter's dialect. They neither perceive the missionaries as a threat nor react violently like the village of Abame, even though the missionaries call their gods "false" outright. And the missionaries do not forcibly thrust Christianity on the villagers.

Considering the emphasis that the Igbo place on careful thought before violent action, Okonkwo's belief that the people of Abame should have armed themselves and killed the white men reflects a rash, violent nature that seems to clash with fundamental Igbo values. Throughout *Things Fall Apart,* Igbo customs and social institutions emphasize the wisdom of seeking a peaceful solution to conflict before a violent solution. Uchendu voices this social value when he states that the killing of the first white man was foolish, for the villagers of Abame did not even know what the man's intentions were.

The language that Achebe uses to describe the pleasure that Nwoye finds in Christianity reflects Umuofia's seeming need to be soothed physically as well as spiritually. Achebe sets up, from the beginning of the novel, a system of images that accentuate both the dry land and the tense atmosphere in the village. The image of the words of the hymn as raindrops relieving Nwoye's "parched soul" refers not only to relief from the arid, desertlike heat with which Africa is commonly associated but also to the act of bringing Nwoye out of his supposed ignorance and into enlightenment through Christianity. It begins to quench his thirst for answers that Igbo religion has not been able to provide him.

CHAPTERS SEVENTEEN–NINETEEN

SUMMARY: CHAPTER SEVENTEEN

The missionaries request a piece of land on which to build a church. The village leaders and elders offer them a plot in the Evil Forest, believing that the missionaries will not accept it. To the elders' amazement, the missionaries rejoice in the offer. But the elders are certain that the forest's sinister spirits and forces will kill the missionaries within days. To their surprise, however, nothing happens, and the church soon wins its first three converts. The villagers point out that sometimes their ancestral spirits will allow an offending man a grace period of twenty-eight days before they punish his sins, but they are completely astounded when nothing happens after twenty-eight days. The church thus wins more converts, including a pregnant woman, Nneka. Her four previous pregnancies produced twins, and her husband and his family are not sorry to see her go.

One of Okonkwo's cousins notices Nwoye among the Christians and informs Okonkwo. When Nwoye returns, Okonkwo chokes him by the neck, demanding to know where he has been. Uchendu orders him to let go of the boy. Nwoye leaves his father's compound and travels to a school in Umuofia to learn reading and writing. Okonkwo wonders how he could ever have fathered such an effeminate, weak son.

SUMMARY: CHAPTER EIGHTEEN

The church wins many converts from the *efulefu,* titleless, worthless men. One day, several *osu,* or outcasts, come to church. Many of the converts move away from them, though they do not leave the service. Afterward, there is an uproar, but Mr. Kiaga firmly refuses to deny the outcasts membership in the church. He argues that they will not die if they cut their hair or break any of the other taboos that have been imposed upon them. Mr. Kiaga's steadfast conviction persuades most of the other converts not to reject their new faith simply because the outcasts have joined them. The *osu* soon become the most zealous members of the church. To the clan's disbelief, one boasts that he killed the sacred royal python. Okonkwo urges Mbanta to drive the Christians out with violence, but the rulers and elders decide to ostracize them instead. Okonkwo bitterly remarks that this is a "womanly" clan. After announcing the new policy of ostracism, the elders learn that the man who boasted of killing the snake has died of an illness. The villagers' trust in their gods is thereby reaffirmed, and they cease to ostracize the converts.

SUMMARY: CHAPTER NINETEEN

Okonkwo's seven years of exile in Mbanta are drawing to an end. Before he returns to Umuofia, he provides a large feast for his mother's kinsmen. He is grateful to them but secretly regrets the missed opportunity to have increased further his status and influence among his own clan. He also regrets having spent time with such un-masculine people. At the feast, one man expresses surprise that Okonkwo has been so generous with his food and another praises Okonkwo's devotion to the kinship bond. He also expresses concern for the younger generation, as Christianity is winning people away from their families and traditions.

ANALYSIS: CHAPTERS SEVENTEEN–NINETEEN

Nwoye is drawn to Christianity because it seems to answer his long-held doubts about his native religion, specifically the abandonment of twin newborns and Ikemefuna's death. Furthermore, Nwoye feels himself exiled from his society because of his disbelief in its laws, and the church offers refuge to those whom society has cast out. The church's value system will allow twins to live, for example, which offers comfort to the pregnant woman who has had to endure the casting away to die of her four sets of newborn twins. Similarly, men without titles turn to Christianity to find affirmation of their individual worth. The *osu* are able to discard others' perception of them as members of an ostracized caste and enter the church as the equals of other converts.

Okonkwo, on the other hand, has good reason to reject Christianity. Should Mbanta not drive the missionaries away, his killing of Ikemefuna would lose part of its religious justification. The damage to his relationship with Nwoye also seems more pointless than before. Both matters become his mistake rather than the result of divine will. Moreover, men of high status like Okonkwo view the church as a threat because it undermines the cultural value of their accomplishments. Their titles and their positions as religious authorities and clan leaders lose force and prestige if men of lower status are not there—the great cannot be measured against the worthless if the worthless have disappeared.

Nwoye's conversion devastates Okonkwo. Although he has always been harsh with his son, Okonkwo still believes in Nwoye's potential to become a great clansman. Nwoye's rejection of Igbo values, however, strikes a dire blow to Okonkwo's hopes for him. Additionally, Nwoye's actions undermine Okonkwo's own status and prestige. It is, as Okonkwo thinks at the end of Chapter Seventeen, as though all of Okonkwo's hard work to distance himself from the legacy of his father has been destroyed. He sighs and thinks to himself: "Living fire begets cold impotent ash."

Despite the challenges that the church represents, Mbanta is committed to peace and remains tolerant of the church's presence. Even with the converts' blatant disrespect of Umuofia's customs—rumor has it that a convert has killed a royal python—the clan leaders vote for a peaceful solution, deciding to ostracize rather than attack the Christians. Okonkwo is not happy with their decision and advocates a violent reaction. His mentality is somewhat ironic:

he believes that the village should act against its cultural values in order to preserve them.

The arrival of the white colonists and their religion weakens the kinship bonds so central to Igbo culture. Ancestral worship plays an important role in Igbo religion, and conversion to Christianity involves a partial rejection of the Igbo structure of kinship. The Christians tell the Igbo that they are all brothers and sons of God, replacing the literal ties of kinship with a metaphorical kinship structure through God. The overjoyed response of a missionary to Nwoye's interest in attending school in another village—"Blessed is he who forsakes his father and his mother for my sake"—illustrates that the Christian church clearly recognizes Igbo kinship bonds as the central obstacle to the success of its missionaries.

Achebe does not present a clear-cut dichotomy of the white religion as evil and the Igbo religion as good. All along, the descriptions of many of the village's ceremonies and rituals have been tongue-in-cheek. But the Christian missionaries increasingly win converts simply by pointing out the fallacy of Igbo beliefs—for example, those about the outcasts. When the outcasts cut their hair with no negative consequence, many villagers come to believe that the Christian god is more powerful than their own. Achebe himself is the son of Nigerian Christians, and it is hard not to think of his situation, in Chapter Seventeen, when the narrator points out Okonkwo's worry: "Suppose when he died all his male children decided to follow Nwoye's steps and abandon their ancestors?"

CHAPTERS TWENTY–TWENTY-ONE

How do you think we can fight when our own brothers have turned against us?

(See QUOTATIONS, p. 52)

SUMMARY: CHAPTER TWENTY

Okonkwo has planned since his first year in exile to rebuild his compound on a larger scale. He also wants to take two more wives and get titles for his sons. He has managed to get over Nwoye's disgraceful departure, but he still regrets that Ezinma is a girl. He asked that she wait to marry in Umuofia, after his exile, to which she consented. She even persuaded her sister, Obiageli, to do the same. Okonkwo hopes to attract interest when he returns with two beautiful, marriageable daughters.

However, Umuofia is much changed after seven years. The church has grown in strength and the white men subject the villagers to their judicial system and rules of government. They are harsh and arrogant, and Okonkwo cannot believe that his clan has not driven the white men and their church out. Sorrowfully, Obierika explains that the church has weakened the ties of kinship and that it is too late to drive the white men out. Many of the clansmen are now on the white man's side. Okonkwo observes that the white man is very shrewd because he came in peace and appeared to have only benevolent interests in the Africans, who thus permitted him to stay. They discuss the story of Aneto, who was hanged by the government after he killed a man with whom he had a dispute. Aneto had been unsatisfied with the new court's ruling on the dispute because it ignored custom. Obierika and Okonkwo conclude their discussion on a fatalistic note, sitting in silence together.

SUMMARY: CHAPTER TWENTY-ONE
Many people of Umuofia are not entirely unhappy with the white men's influence on their community. They have set up trading posts, and money is flowing into the village. Mr. Brown, the white missionary, restrains his flock from antagonizing the clan. He and Akunna, one of the clan's leaders, meet often to debate and discuss their respective religious views. Akunna explains that the clan also has just one god, Chukwu, who created the world and the other gods. Mr. Brown replies that there are no other gods. He points to a carving and states that it is not a god but a piece of wood. Akunna agrees that it is a piece of wood, but wood created by Chukwu. Neither converts the other, but each leaves with a greater understanding of the other's faith.

Mr. Brown builds a hospital and a school. He begs the villagers to send their children to school and warns them that if they do not, strangers who can read and write will come to rule them. His arguments are fairly effective and his hospital wins praise for its treatments. When Okonkwo first returns to Umuofia, Mr. Brown goes to tell him that Nwoye is in a training college for teachers. Okonkwo chases him away with threats of violence. Not long afterward, Mr. Brown's health begins to fail, and, sad, he leaves his flock.

Okonkwo's daughters attract many suitors, but to his grave disappointment, his clan takes no particular interest in his return. The ozo initiation ceremony occurs only once in three years, meaning that he must wait two years to initiate his sons. He deeply regrets the changes in his once warlike people.

ANALYSIS: CHAPTERS TWENTY–TWENTY-ONE

Okonkwo's status as a warrior and farmer and his clan's perception of him have changed since his exile. His increasing loss of power and prestige brings him great anxiety. Any remaining doubt that Okonkwo is slightly crazy is quelled when we learn that he has been fantasizing about, and seriously planning for, his triumphant return to his village since his departure. Okonkwo has great expectations for himself—in Chapter Twenty we are told that, "he saw himself taking the highest title of the land."

Although Okonkwo still wishes that Ezinma were a boy, she remains a comfort to him throughout his troubles. Ironically, she best understands the dilemma of compromised manhood that her father faces. She sees how important her marriage is to Okonkwo's position in the community, and she has considerable influence over her sister, who quickly agrees to postpone her marriage as well. After Nwoye's departure, Okonkwo shows no sign of changing his practice of lecturing his sons about the rash and violent nature of true masculinity, showing his continued refusal to accept the fact that aggressiveness and pensiveness are not gender-defined, mutually exclusive traits.

Already having dealt with the missionaries in Mbanta, Okonkwo is now forced to deal with them in his own village. However, Mr. Brown, their leader, is far more enlightened than the average white colonist. Although he doesn't really understand Igbo beliefs, he is capable of respecting them, and he does not want his flock to antagonize the clan. In a rare occurrence of cross-cultural understanding, he seems to share the clan's value of peaceful, harmonious relations, and he debates religion with Akunna without insults or violence. His influence is largely benevolent, and Achebe uses Mr. Brown as a foil for the missionary who eventually takes his place, the more radical Reverend Smith.

Things Fall Apart is not one-sided in its portrayal of colonialism. It presents the economic benefits of cross-cultural contact and reveals the villagers' delight in the hospital's treatment of illnesses. The sympathetic Mr. Brown urges the Igbo to send their children to school because he knows that the colonial government will rob the Igbo of self-government if they do not know the language. In essence, he urges the Igbo to adapt so that they won't lose all autonomy. Nevertheless, it is difficult to view colonialism in a tremendously positive light: suddenly the Igbo must relate to the colonial government on European terms. The story of Abame and the discussion of the new judicial system show how different the European frame of reference is from that of the *egwugwu*. The colonial government punishes individuals according to European cultural and religious values. For example, without first making an effort to understand the cultural and religious tradition behind the practice, the government pronounces the abandonment of newborn twins a punishable crime.

At the end of Chapter Twenty, Obierika points out that there is no way that the white man will be able to understand Umuofia's customs without understanding its language. This idea mirrors one of Achebe's purposes in writing *Things Fall Apart*: the book serves not only to remind the West that Africa has language and culture but also to provide an understanding of Igbo culture through language. Achebe shows us the extent to which cultural and linguistic structures and practices are intertwined, and he is able to re-create in English the cadences, images, and rhythms of the speech of the Igbo people. By the time things begin to "fall apart," it becomes clear that what the colonialists have unraveled is the complex Igbo culture.

CHAPTERS TWENTY-TWO–TWENTY-THREE

SUMMARY: CHAPTER TWENTY-TWO

Reverend James Smith, a strict and intolerant man, replaces Mr. Brown. He demands the utmost obedience to the letter of the Bible and disapproves of Mr. Brown's tolerant and unorthodox policies. The more zealous converts are relieved to be free of Mr. Brown's policy of restraint. One such convert, Enoch, dares to unmask an *egwugwu* during the annual ceremony to honor the earth deity, an act equivalent to killing an ancestral spirit. The next day, the *egwugwu* burn Enoch's compound to the ground. They then gather in front of the church to confront Reverend Smith and his fellow Christians. They tell the Christians that they only wish to destroy the church in order to cleanse their village of Enoch's horrible sin. Smith replies that he will stand his ground. He forbids them to touch the church, but his interpreter alters Smith's statement for fear that the unvarnished truth will be too harsh and that he will suffer as the messenger of bad news. He tells the *egwugwu* that Smith demands that they leave the matter in his hands. They ignore Smith's orders and burn the church.

SUMMARY: CHAPTER TWENTY-THREE

Okonkwo is almost happy again, despite the fact that his clan did not agree to kill the Christians or drive them away. Even so, he and the rest of the villagers are on their guard, and for the next two days they arm themselves with guns and machetes. The District Commissioner returns from his tour and requests that the leaders of Umuofia meet with him. They go, taking only their machetes because guns would be "unseemly." The commissioner talks to them in condescending terms and says that they should discuss the church's burning "as friends." No sooner have they put their machetes on the floor than a group of soldiers surprises them. They are handcuffed and thrown in jail for several days, where they suffer insults and physical abuse. A kind of bail is set at two hundred bags of cowries. The court messengers tell the people of Umuofia that they must pay a fine of two hundred and fifty bags of cowries or their leaders will be hanged—by upping the price these messengers will make a profit as intermediaries. The town crier announces an emergency village meeting. Even Ezinma returns home from her twenty-eight-day visit to her future in-laws. The next morning they decide to collect the cowries necessary to pay the fine.

ANALYSIS: CHAPTERS TWENTY-TWO–TWENTY-THREE

Reverend Smith causes a great deal of conflict between the church and the clan with his refusal to understand and respect traditional Igbo culture. Mr. Brown, by contrast, is far more lenient with the converts' retention of some of their old beliefs and doesn't draw as clear a line between the converts and the Igbo community. Smith, however, demands a complete rejection of the converts' old religious beliefs. The text ironically comments that he "sees things as black and white." While on the one hand this comment refers simply to an inability to grasp the gradations in a given situation, it also refers, of course, to race relations and colonial power. Interestingly, Achebe has named Smith's predecessor "Brown," as if to suggest that the latter's practice of compromise and benevolence is in some way related to his ability to see the shades between the poles of black and white. Smith, by contrast, is a stereotypical European colonialist, as the generic quality of his name reflects. His inability to practice mutual respect and tolerance incites a dangerous zealous fervor in some of the more eager converts, such as Enoch. Smith's attitude encourages Enoch to insult traditional Igbo culture.

That Enoch is the son of the snake-priest makes his suspected killing of the sacred python all the more dire a transgression. Enoch's conversion and alleged attack on the python emblematize the transition from the old order to the new. The old religion, with its insistence on deism and animal worship, is overturned from within by one. In its place comes the new religion, which, for all its protestations of love and harmony, brandishes a fiery logic and fierce resolve to convert the Igbo at any cost.

Enoch figures as a double for Okonkwo, although they espouse different beliefs. They are similar in temperament, and each man rebels against the practices and legacies of his father. Like Okonkwo, Enoch feels above all others in his tradition. He also feels contempt for them—he imagines that every sermon is "preached for the benefit of his enemies," and, in the middle of church, he gives knowing looks whenever he feels that his superiority has been affirmed. Most important, in his blind and unthinking adherence to Christianity, Enoch allows his violent desires to take over, just as Okonkwo is prone to do.

The language barrier between the colonists and the villagers enables a crucial misunderstanding to take place. Unawareness of his interpreter's attempt to appease the villagers, Smith considers the burning of the church an open show of disrespect for the church and his authority. The power that the interpreter holds highlights the weaknesses and vulnerability created by the language gap, reinforcing Mr. Brown's belief that reading and writing are essential skills for the villagers if they hope to maintain their autonomy. This miscommunication reminds us of Parrot's trickiness in Ekwefi's story about Tortoise.

Okonkwo's desire to respond violently to the Christian church is not completely motivated by a desire to preserve his clan's cultural traditions. He has been fantasizing for many years about making a big splash with his return to his village, but the church has changed things so much that his return fails to incite the interest that he has anticipated. He has also hoped that his daughters' marriages would help to bring him some reflected glory but, again, his daughters' suitors did not cause Umuofia to notice him. The opportunity to once again be a warrior represents Okonkwo's last chance to recapture some of his former glory. His motivations for wanting revenge, including his humiliation in the jail, are deeply personal.

Chapters Twenty-Four–Twenty-Five

Summary: Chapter Twenty-Four

After their release, the prisoners return to the village with such brooding looks that the women and children from the village are afraid to greet them. The whole village is overcome with a tense and unnatural silence. Ezinma takes Okonkwo some food, and she and Obierika notice the whip marks on his back.

The village crier announces another meeting for the following morning, and the clan is filled with a sense of foreboding. At sunrise, the villagers gather. Okonkwo has slept very little out of excitement and anticipation. He has thought it over and decided on a course of action to which he will stick no matter what the village decides as a whole. He takes out his war dress and assesses his smoked raffia skirt, tall feather headgear, and shield as in adequate condition. He remembers his former glories in battle and ponders that the nature of man has changed. The meeting is packed with men from all of the clan's nine villages.

The first speaker laments the damage that the white man and his church have done to the clan and bewails the desecration of the gods and ancestral spirits. He reminds the clan that it may have to spill clansmen's blood if it enters into battle with the white men. In the middle of the speech, five court messengers approach the crowd. Their leader orders the meeting to end. No sooner have the words left the messenger's mouth than Okonkwo kills him with two strokes of his machete. A tumult rises in the crowd, but not the kind for which Okonkwo hopes: the villagers allow the messengers to escape and bring the meeting to a conclusion. Someone even asks why Okonkwo killed the messenger. Understanding that his clan will not go to war, Okonkwo wipes his machete free of blood and departs.

> *He had already chosen the title of the book . . . The*
> *Pacification of the Primitive Tribes of the Lower Niger.*
> (See QUOTATIONS, p. 51)

Summary: Chapter Twenty-Five

When the District Commissioner arrives at Okonkwo's compound, he finds a small group of men sitting outside. He asks for Okonkwo, and the men tell him that Okonkwo is not at home. The commissioner asks a second time, and Obierika repeats his initial answer. The commissioner starts to get angry and threatens to imprison them all if they do not cooperate. Obierika agrees to lead him to Okonkwo in return for some assistance. Although the commissioner does not understand the gist of the exchange, he follows Obierika and a group of clansmen. They proceed to a small bush behind Okonkwo's compound, where they discover Okonkwo's body dangling from a tree. He has hanged himself.

Obierika explains that suicide is a grave sin and his clansmen may not touch Okonkwo's body. Though they have sent for strangers from a distant village to help take the body down, they also ask the commissioner for help. He asks why they cannot do it themselves, and they explain that his body is evil now and that only strangers may touch it. They are not allowed to bury it, but again, strangers can. Obierika displays an uncharacteristic flash of temper and lashes out at the commissioner, blaming him for Okonkwo's death and praising his friend's greatness. The commissioner decides to honor the group's request, but he leaves and orders his messengers to do the work. As he departs, he congratulates himself for having added to his store of knowledge of African customs.

The commissioner, who is in the middle of writing a book about Africa, imagines that the circumstances of Okonkwo's death will make an interesting paragraph or two, if not an entire chapter. He has already chosen the title: *The Pacification of the Primitive Tribes of the Lower Niger.*

ANALYSIS: CHAPTERS TWENTY-FOUR–TWENTY-FIVE

It is in Okonkwo's nature to act rashly, and his slaying of the messenger constitutes an instinctive act of self-preservation. Not to act would be to reject his values and traditional way of life. He cannot allow himself or, by extension, his clan to be viewed as cowardly. There is certainly an element of self-destructiveness in this act, a kind of martyrdom that Okonkwo willingly embraces because the alternative is to submit to a world, law, and new order with which he finds himself inexorably at odds.

Unoka's words regarding the bitterness of failing alone come to have real significance in Okonkwo's life. In fact, they can be seen as a fatalistic foreshadowing of the bitter losses that befall Okonkwo despite his efforts to distance himself from his father's model of indolence and irresponsibility. He values his personal success and status over the survival of the community and, having risen to the top of the clan's economic and political heap alone, he fails alone. Okonkwo's lack of concern for the fate of his community is manifested when, before the clan-wide meeting, he doesn't bother to exchange greetings with anyone. He is not interested in the fate of anyone other than himself. Despite his great success and prestige, he dies in ignominy like his titleless, penniless father. This solitude persists even after his life ends, as the supposed taking over of his body by evil spirits renders his clan unable to handle his burial.

One way of understanding Okonkwo's suicide is as the result of a self-fulfilling prophecy regarding his fear of failure. He is so afraid of ending up precisely the way he does end up that he brings about his own end in the worst manner imaginable. No one forces his hand when he slays the messenger; rather, the act constitutes a desperate attempt to reassert his manhood. The great tragedy of the situation is that Okonkwo ignores far more effective but less masculine ways to resist the colonialists. Ultimately, Okonkwo's sacrifice seems futile and empty.

The novel's ending is dark and ironic. The District Commissioner is a pompous little man who thinks that he understands indigenous African cultures. Achebe uses the commissioner, who seems a character straight out of *Heart of Darkness,* to demonstrate the inaccuracy of accounts of Africa such as Joseph Conrad's. The commissioner's misinterpretations and the degree to which they are based upon his own shortcomings are evident. He comments, for example, on the villagers' "love of superfluous words," attempting to ridicule their beautiful and expressive language. His rumination that Okonkwo's story could make for a good paragraph illustrates his shallowness. Whereas Achebe has written an entire book about Okonkwo, he suggests that a European account of Okonkwo would likely portray him as a grunting, cultureless savage who inexplicably and senselessly kills a messenger. Achebe also highlights one of the reasons that early ethnographic reports were often offensively inaccurate: when Obierika asks the commissioner to help him with Okonkwo's body, the narrator tells us that "the resolute administrator in [the commissioner] gave way to the student of primitive customs." The same people who control the natives relay the accepted accounts of colonized cultures—in a manner, of course, that best suits the colonizer's interest.

Achebe's novel seeks at least in part to provide an answer to such inaccurate stereotypes. Okonkwo is by no means perfect. One can argue that his tragedy is of his own making. One can also argue that his *chi* is to blame. But as a societal tragedy, *Things Fall Apart* obviously places no blame on the Igbo people for the colonialism to which they were subjected. At the same time, the traditional customs of the villagers are not glorified—they are often questioned or criticized. Achebe's re-creation of the complexity of Okonkwo's and Umuofia's situations lends a fairness to his writing. At the same time, his critique of colonialism and of colonial literary representations comes across loud and clear.

IMPORTANT QUOTATIONS EXPLAINED

1. Turning and turning in the widening gyre
    The falcon cannot hear the falconer;
    Things fall apart; the center cannot hold;
    Mere anarchy is loosed upon the world.

Achebe uses this opening stanza of William Butler Yeats's poem "The Second Coming," from which the title of the novel is taken, as an epigraph to the novel. In invoking these lines, Achebe hints at the chaos that arises when a system collapses. That "the center cannot hold" is an ironic reference to both the imminent collapse of the African tribal system, threatened by the rise of imperialist bureaucracies, and the imminent disintegration of the British Empire. Achebe, writing in 1959, had the benefit of retrospection in depicting Nigerian society and British colonialism in the 1890s.

Yet Achebe's allusion is not simply political, nor is it ironic on only one level. Yeats's poem is about the Second Coming, a return and revelation of sorts. In Things Fall Apart, this revelation refers to the advent of the Christian missionaries (and the alleged revelation of their teachings), further satirizing their supposed benevolence in converting the Igbo. For an agricultural society accustomed to a series of cycles, including that of the locusts, the notion of return would be quite credible and familiar.

The hyperbolic and even contradictory nature of the passage's language suggests the inability of humankind to thwart this collapse. "Mere anarchy" is an oxymoron in a sense, since the definition of anarchy implies an undeniably potent level of radicalism. The abstraction in the language makes the poem's ideas universal: by referring to "[t]hings" falling apart as opposed to specifying what those collapsing or disintegrating things are, Yeats (and Achebe) leaves his words open to a greater range of interpretations. It is worth noting, in addition, that Achebe cuts away from the poem just as it picks up its momentum and begins to speak of "innocence drowned" and "blood-dimmed" tides. It is a measure of Achebe's subtlety that he prefers a prologue that is understated and suggestive, rather than polemical, ranting, and violent.

2.　　And at last the locusts did descend. They settled on every
　　　　tree and on every blade of grass; they settled on the roofs and
　　　　covered the bare ground. Mighty tree branches broke away
　　　　under them, and the whole country became the brown-earth
　　　　color of the vast, hungry swarm.

This passage from Chapter Seven represents, in highly allegorical
terms, the arrival of the colonizers. The locusts have been coming
for years, but their symbolic significance in this passage lies in the
inevitable arrival of the colonizers, which will alter the landscape
and psychology of the Igbo people irreparably. The repetition of the
phrase "They settled," an example of the rhetorical device ana-
phora (in which a clause begins with the same word or words with
which the previous clause begins), in addition to the repetition of the
word "every," reflects the suddenly ubiquitous presence of the
locusts. The choice of the verb "settle," of course, clearly refers to
the colonizers. The branches that break under the weight of the
locusts are symbols of the traditions and cultural roots of Igbo society,
which can no longer survive under the onslaught of colonialism and
white settlement. Ironically, the "vast, hungry swarm" is not white but
rather brown like the earth; the emphasis, however, remains on the
locusts' consumptive nature and inescapable presence.

3.　　Among the Igbo the art of conversation is regarded very
　　　　highly, and proverbs are the palm-oil with which words are
　　　　eaten.

This quote, from the narrator's recounting, in Chapter One, of how
Unoka calmly interacted with someone to whom he owed money,
alludes to the highly sophisticated art of rhetoric practiced by the
Igbo. This rhetorical formalness offers insight into the misunder-
standings that occur between the Igbo and the Europeans. Whereas
the latter value efficiency and directness in their dealings, the Igbo
value an adherence to their cultural traditions, which include certain patterns of dialogue considered inefficient by Western standards. The metaphor of words as food is highly appropriate, given
the almost exclusively agricultural nature of Igbo society. They
award the same value that they place on food, the sustenance of life,
to words, the sustenance of interaction and hence community.

4. He had already chosen the title of the book, after much thought: The Pacification of the Primitive Tribes of the Lower Niger.

This sentence, which concludes the novel, satirizes the entire tradition of western ethnography and imperialism itself as a cultural project, and it suggests that the ethnographer in question, the District Commissioner, knows very little about his subject and projects a great deal of his European colonialist values onto it. The language of the commissioner's proposed title reveals how misguided he is: that he thinks of himself as someone who knows a great deal about pacifying the locals is highly ironic, since, in fact, he is a primary source of their distress, not their peace. Additionally, the notion of "[p]acification" is inherently offensive—a condescending conception of the natives as little more than helpless infants. Similarly, the label "[p]rimitive" comes across as a patronizing insult that reflects the commissioner's ignorance about the Igbo and their complexly ritualized and highly formalized mode of life. The assertion that the commissioner has come up with a title "after much thought" accentuates the fact that the level of attention he has paid to his own thoughts and perceptions well exceeds that paid to the actual subject of the study.

5.   "Does the white man understand our custom about land?"
     "How can he when he does not even speak our tongue? But
     he says that our customs are bad; and our own brothers who
     have taken up his religion also say that our customs are bad.
     How do you think we can fight when our own brothers have
     turned against us? The white man is very clever. He came
     quietly and peaceably with his religion. We were amused at
     his foolishness and allowed him to stay. Now he has won
     our brothers, and our clan can no longer act like one. He has
     put a knife on the things that held us together and we have
     fallen apart."

This exchange occurs at the end of Chapter Twenty during the conversation between Obierika and Okonkwo. In the discussion, which
centers on various events that have come to pass since the arrival of
the colonialists, Obierika seems to voice Achebe's own thoughts on
colonialism. Upset by the fact that the white men have come and
completely disregarded the Igbo sense of justice, Obierika points
out the impossibility of the colonialists understanding anything
about the Umuofians without speaking their language. He points
out the ludicrousness of denigrating unfamiliar customs.

   Yet, Obierika does not lay the blame wholly on the side of the
white man. He feels also that the Umuofians who have converted to
Christianity have consciously and wrongly turned their backs on
their own "brothers." This assessment complicates our understanding of the novel, as Achebe prevents us from seeing matters in clear-
cut terms of good (black) versus bad (white). Indeed, Achebe else-
where attempts to demonstrate the validity of some questions about
Igbo culture and tradition. If religion and tradition are the threads
that hold the clan together, and if that religion is flawed and that tradition vulnerable, it becomes hard to determine who is at fault for the
resulting destruction. Certainly, Achebe does not blame the villagers.
But, while this quotation displays his condemnation of the colonialists
for their disrespect toward Igbo customs, it also shows his criticism of
some clan members' responses to the colonial presence.

KEY FACTS

FULL TITLE
Things Fall Apart

AUTHOR
Chinua Achebe

TYPE OF WORK
Novel

GENRE
Postcolonial critique; tragedy

LANGUAGE
English

TIME AND PLACE WRITTEN
1959, Nigeria

DATE OF FIRST PUBLICATION
1959

PUBLISHER
Heinemann Educational Books

NARRATOR
The narrator is anonymous but shows sympathy for the various residents of Umuofia.

POINT OF VIEW
The narration is in the third person, by an omniscient figure who focuses on Okonkwo but switches from character to character to detail the thoughts and motives of various individuals.

TONE
Ironic, tragic, satirical, fablelike

TENSE
Past

SETTING (TIME)
1890s

SETTING (PLACE)
Lower Nigerian villages, Iguedo and Mbanta in particular

PROTAGONIST
Okonkwo

MAJOR CONFLICT
On one level, the conflict is between the traditional society of Umuofia and the new customs brought by the whites, which are in turn adopted by many of the villagers. Okonkwo also struggles to be as different from his deceased father as possible. He believes his father to have been weak, effeminate, lazy, ignominious, and poor. Consequently, Okonkwo strives to be strong, masculine, industrious, respected, and wealthy.

RISING ACTION
Enoch's unmasking of an egwugwu, the egwugwu's burning of the church, and the District Commissioner's sneaky arrest of Umuofian leaders force the tension between Umuofia and the colonizers to a breaking point.

CLIMAX
Okonkwo's murder, or uchu, of a court messenger

FALLING ACTION
The villagers allow the white government's messengers to escape and Okonkwo, realizing the weakness of his clan, commits suicide.

THEMES
The struggle between tradition and change; varying interpretations of masculinity; language as a sign of cultural difference

MOTIFS
Chi, animal imagery

SYMBOLS
The novel is highly symbolic, and it asks to be read in symbolic terms. Two of the main symbols are the locusts and fire. The locusts symbolize the white colonists descending upon the Africans, seeming to augur good but actually portending troublesome encounters. Fire epitomizes Okonkwo's nature—he is fierce and destructive. A third symbol, the drums, represents the physical connection of the community of clansmen in

Umuofia, and acts as a metaphorical heartbeat that beats in
unison, uniting all the village members.

FORESHADOWING

The author's initial description of Ikemefuna as an "ill-fated
boy," which presages his eventual murder by Okonkwo; the
arrival of the locusts, which symbolizes the eventual arrival of
the colonizers; Obierika's suggestion that Okonkwo kill himself,
which foretells Okonkwo's eventual suicide

STUDY QUESTIONS & ESSAY TOPICS

STUDY QUESTIONS

1. *Why does* THINGS FALL APART *end with the District Commissioner musing about the book that he is writing on Africa?*

The novel's ending is Achebe's most potent satirical stab at the tradition of Western ethnography. At the end of Okonkwo's story, Achebe alludes to the lack of depth and sensitivity with which the Europeans will inevitably treat Okonkwo's life. Achebe shows that a book such as *The Pacification of the Primitive Tribes of the Lower Niger,* which the commissioner plans to write, reveals much more about the writers—the colonialists—than about the subjects supposedly being studied. The title of the book is also ironic, as it reflects the utter lack of communication between the Europeans and the Africans. Although the Commissioner thinks he has achieved the "[p]acification" of these tribes, he has only contributed to their unrest and increasing lack of peace.

Additionally, the artifice of wrapping up the narrative as fodder for an ethnographic study hearkens back to the close of Joseph Conrad's *Heart of Darkness.* As Marlow, the teller of the main story in *Heart of Darkness,* concludes his tale about colonization in Africa, the initial narrator, waiting with Marlow to sail out to sea, returns and ponders the water, leaving the reader to wonder what atrocities beyond those in Marlow's story the British Empire will commit. The conclusion of *Things Fall Apart* gives the impression of a similar story-within-a-story structure. When the account of how the colonizers have imposed themselves upon Umuofia concludes, the commissioner contemplates the account, leaving little doubt that he will now proceed to impose European values on his version of the account.

2.   *What is the nature of Okonkwo's relationship with Ezinma?*

Although Okonkwo is generally misogynistic, his favorite child is his daughter Ezinma. Of all Okonkwo's children, Ezinma best understands how to handle her father's anger. One example of her sensitivity to his needs is her comforting of him after he has killed Ikemefuna. Ezinma can tell that Okonkwo is depressed but, not wanting to upset him, she doesn't address his sorrow directly. Instead, she brings him food and urges him to eat. His frequent remarks that he wishes Ezinma were his son because she has the "right spirit" suggest that he desires an affectionate attachment with his sons, so long as it is not openly shown or acknowledged. He values Ezinma not because she exhibits desirable masculine traits but because of their tacit bond of sympathy and understanding.

3.   *What does the repetition of the number seven suggest about the novel?*

In several places (Mr. Brown's conversations with Akunna, for example), the novel explicitly focuses on the theological and moral similarities between Christianity and Igbo religion. The repetition of the number seven—symbolically important to both religions—is another way of highlighting the similarities between the two cultures. The text seems to draw a parallel between the apparent randomness of the symbolic number often chosen by the Igbo and the determinism of Christianity's reliance on the number seven in the Bible and in the myth of creation. Indeed, the text explicitly refers to resting on the seventh day; this return to the number seven marks a similarity between the two cultures' belief systems.

SUGGESTED ESSAY TOPICS

1. *Think about the role of weather in the novel. How does it work, symbolically or otherwise, in relation to important elements of the novel such as religion? Are rain and draught significant? Explore the ways in which weather affects the emotional and spiritual realms of the novel as well as the physical world.*

2. *Women suffer great losses in this novel but also, in certain circumstances, hold tremendous power. What role do women play in Okonkwo's life? Is there any difference between his interaction with specific women and his understanding of women and femininity in general?*

3. *Animal imagery abounds in the folktales and proverbs circulated among the clan members. What is the significance of some of the animals they discuss? What does the prominence of animal figures suggest about Igbo culture and about Achebe's larger goals?*

4. *In what ways does the idea of progress shape the novel? If Unoka, Okonkwo, and Nwoye are symbolic of three successive generations, how does society in Umuofia change over the course of their lifetimes? Where does Ikemefuna fit into this picture?*

5. *Throughout the novel, drums, music, and the town crier's voice punctuate the narrative at key moments. When does silence occur and what does it mean? Is there more than one type of silence? Can silence be characterized as a positive or negative occurrence? What are the implications of the fact that Unoka takes his flute with him to the Evil Forest when he dies?*

Review & Resources

Quiz

1. What is the name of Okonkwo's motherland?

   A. Mbaino
   B. Mbutu
   C. Mbanta
   D. Mantra

2. What holy animal does Okonkwo's clan suspect the Christians have killed and eaten?

   A. A locust
   B. A python
   C. A monkey
   D. A tortoise

3. What is the name of the first missionary who comes to Umuofia?

   A. Mr. Brown
   B. Reverend Smith
   C. Mr. Jones
   D. Missionary Man

4. How many villages does Umuofia comprise?

   A. One
   B. Four
   C. Nine
   D. Seven

5. Whom did Okonkwo beat in his legendary wrestling match?

   A. Ekwefi Ogbuedi the Rooster
   B. Ogbuedi the Snake
   C. Isaac the Toad
   D. Amalinze the Cat

6.   In what country does Things Fall Apart take place?

   A.   Kenya
   B.   Nigeria
   C.   Chad
   D.   South Africa

7.   What do the inhabitants of Mbanta believe is responsible for the white man's miraculous survival after having built his church in the Evil Forest?

   A.   His eyeglasses
   B.   His Bible
   C.   His borrowed machete
   D.   His attitude

8.   What is an ogbanje?

   A.   A masked spirit
   B.   A type of yam soup
   C.   A changeling child
   D.   A musical instrument

9.   What does Okonkwo constantly wish Ezinma had been?

   A.   His firstborn child
   B.   A son
   C.   A better cook
   D.   A donkey

10.   What does a palm tapper tap?

   A.   His hand, to keep the beat
   B.   A shoulder, for advice
   C.   A tree, for wine
   D.   The ground, for oil

11.   For what reason is Okonkwo exiled?

   A.   He owes money
   B.   He willfully kills a fellow clan member
   C.   He steals yams
   D.   He unintentionally kills a fellow clan member

12. What are the outcasts required to do before they may join the church?

    A. Shave their heads
    B. Pierce their tongues
    C. Get cam wood tattoos
    D. Change their names

13. What is the name of Okonkwo's second wife?

    A. Chielo
    B. Ojiugo
    C. Ekwefi
    D. Ezinma

14. Where are the Christian women forbidden to go when the clan hears of the killing of a royal python?

    A. To the Evil Forest
    B. To the stream
    C. To the church
    D. To the Tribal Council Meeting

15. What does Okonkwo do even though he is advised not to?

    A. Marry Ojiugo
    B. Beat Nwoye twice
    C. Attack Chielo
    D. Help kill Ikemefuna

16. What crop is king for the Igbo?

    A. Cassava
    B. Yam
    C. Cotton
    D. Riding Crop

17. When the Igbo refer to the "iron-horse," what do they mean?

    A. A train carriage
    B. Maduka, the star wrestler
    C. A bicycle
    D. An elephant

REVIEW & RESOURCES

18. What is the polite name for leprosy among the Igbo?

   A. The swelling sickness
   B. The white skin
   C. The heathen state
   D. The albino condition

19. When do the clan members share the kola nut?

   A. When declaring war
   B. When giving birth to children
   C. When wrestling
   D. When gathering for social occasions

20. In the allegory of Tortoise, what do the birds give to Tortoise?

   A. Bird seed
   B. Feathers
   C. Water
   D. A branch

21. What does Enoch do to provoke the rage of the clan?

   A. He unmasks an egwugwu
   B. He converts Nwoye
   C. He steals 200 cowry shells
   D. He mutilates twins

22. How does Okonkwo die?

   A. He is poisoned by the Commissioner
   B. He hangs himself
   C. He is stabbed by Enoch
   D. He dies of the swelling disease

23. Why are the villagers happy when the locusts arrive?

   A. Because they represent future happiness
   B. Because they mean good weather and good crops
   C. Because their bodies can be made into glue
   D. Because they taste good

24. What does Okonkwo fear most?

    A. Joining the missionaries
    B. Confronting his father
    C. Becoming like his father
    D. The overthrow of the village elders

25. The title *Things Fall Apart* is taken from a poem by

    A. Alfred Lord Tennyson
    B. Joseph Conrad
    C. T.S. Eliot
    D. William Butler Yeats

ANSWER KEY:

1: C; 2: B; 3: A; 4: C; 5: D; 6: B; 7: A; 8: C; 9: B; 10: C; 11: D; 12: A; 13: C; 14: B; 15: D; 16: B; 17: C; 18: B; 19: D; 20: B; 21: A; 22: B; 23: D; 24: C; 25: D

SUGGESTIONS FOR FURTHER READING

ACHEBE, CHINUA, and LINDFORS, BERNTH, ed. *Conversations with Chinua Achebe.* Jackson: University Press of Mississippi, 1997.

———. *Home and Exile.* Oxford: Oxford University Press, 2000.

EZENWA-OHAETO. *Chinua Achebe: A Biography.* Bloomington: Indiana University Press, 1997.

GIKANDI, SIMON. *Reading Chinua Achebe: Language & Ideology in Fiction.* Heinemann, Nairobi: Heinemann Kenya, 1991.

IYASERE, SOLOMON O., ed. *Understanding* THINGS FALL APART: *Selected Essays and Criticism.* Troy, New York: Whitson Publishing, 1998.

KILLAM, G. D. *The Writings of Chinua Achebe.* London: Heinemann Educational, 1977.

OKOYE, EMMANUEL MEZIEMADU. *The Traditional Religion and its Encounter with Christianity in Achebe's Novels.* New York: P. Lang, 1987.

WREN, ROBERT M. *Achebe's World: The Historical and Cultural Context of the Novels of Chinua Achebe.* Essex: Longman, 1980.

REVIEW & RESOURCES

SPARKNOTES
TEST PREPARATION
GUIDES

The SparkNotes team figured it was time to cut standardized tests down to size. We've studied the tests for you, so that SparkNotes test prep guides are:

Smarter:
Packed with critical-thinking skills and test-
taking strategies that will improve your score.

Better:
Fully up to date, covering all new features of the tests,
with study tips on every type of question.

Faster:
Our books cover exactly what you need to
know for the test. No more, no less.

SparkNotes Guide to the SAT & PSAT
SparkNotes Guide to the SAT & PSAT—Deluxe Internet Edition
SparkNotes Guide to the ACT
SparkNotes Guide to the ACT—Deluxe Internet Edition
SparkNotes Guide to the SAT II Writing
SparkNotes Guide to the SAT II U.S. History
SparkNotes Guide to the SAT II Math Ic
SparkNotes Guide to the SAT II Math IIc
SparkNotes Guide to the SAT II Biology
SparkNotes Guide to the SAT II Physics

SparkNotes Literature Guides

1984
The Adventures of
  Huckleberry Finn
The Aeneid
All Quiet on the
  Western Front
And Then There Were
  None
Angela's Ashes
Animal Farm
Anna Karenina
Anne of Green Gables
Anthem
Antony and Cleopatra
As I Lay Dying
As You Like It
Atlas Shrugged
The Awakening
The Autobiography of
  Malcolm X
The Bean Trees
The Bell Jar
Beloved
Beowulf
Billy Budd
Black Boy
Bless Me, Ultima
The Bluest Eye
Brave New World
The Brothers
  Karamazov
The Call of the Wild
Candide
The Canterbury Tales
Catch-22
The Catcher in the Rye
The Chocolate War
The Chosen
Cold Mountain
Cold Sassy Tree
The Color Purple
The Count of Monte
  Cristo
Crime and Punishment
The Crucible
Cry, the Beloved
  Country
Cyrano de Bergerac
David Copperfield
Death of a Salesman
The Death of Socrates

The Diary of a Young
  Girl
A Doll's House
Don Quixote
Dr. Faustus
Dr. Jekyll and Mr. Hyde
Dracula
Dune
Edith Hamilton's
  Mythology
Emma
Ethan Frome
Fahrenheit 451
Fallen Angels
A Farewell to Arms
Farewell to Manzanar
Flowers for Algernon
For Whom the Bell
  Tolls
The Fountainhead
Frankenstein
The Giver
The Glass Menagerie
Gone With the Wind
The Good Earth
The Grapes of Wrath
Great Expectations
The Great Gatsby
Grendel
Gulliver's Travels
Hamlet
The Handmaid's Tale
Hard Times
Harry Potter and the
  Sorcerer's Stone
Heart of Darkness
Henry IV, Part I
Henry V
Hiroshima
The Hobbit
The House of Seven
  Gables
I Know Why the Caged
  Bird Sings
The Iliad
Inferno
Inherit the Wind
Invisible Man
Jane Eyre
Johnny Tremain
The Joy Luck Club

Julius Caesar
The Jungle
The Killer Angels
King Lear
The Last of the
  Mohicans
Les Miserables
A Lesson Before Dying
The Little Prince
Little Women
Lord of the Flies
The Lord of the Rings
Macbeth
Madame Bovary
A Man for All Seasons
The Mayor of
  Casterbridge
The Merchant of Venice
A Midsummer Night's
  Dream
Moby Dick
Much Ado About
  Nothing
My Antonia
Narrative of the Life of
  Frederick Douglass
Native Son
The New Testament
Nicomachean Ethics
Night
Notes from
  Underground
The Odyssey
The Oedipus Plays
Of Mice and Men
The Old Man and the
  Sea
The Old Testament
Oliver Twist
The Once and Future
  King
One Day in the Life of
  Ivan Denisovich
One Flew Over the
  Cuckoo's Nest
One Hundred Years of
  Solitude
Othello
Our Town
The Outsiders
Paradise Lost

A Passage to India
The Pearl
The Picture of Dorian
  Gray
Poe's Short Stories
A Portrait of the Artist
  as a Young Man
Pride and Prejudice
The Prince
A Raisin in the Sun
The Red Badge of
  Courage
The Republic
Richard III
Robinson Crusoe
Romeo and Juliet
The Scarlet Letter
A Separate Peace
Silas Marner
Sir Gawain and the
  Green Knight
Slaughterhouse-Five
Snow Falling on Cedars
Song of Solomon
The Sound and the Fury
Steppenwolf
The Stranger
Streetcar Named
  Desire
The Sun Also Rises
A Tale of Two Cities
The Taming of the
  Shrew
The Tempest
Tess of the d'Ubervilles
Their Eyes Were
  Watching God
Things Fall Apart
The Things They
  Carried
To Kill a Mockingbird
To the Lighthouse
Tom Sawyer
Treasure Island
Twelfth Night
Ulysses
Uncle Tom's Cabin
Walden
War and Peace
Wuthering Heights
A Yellow Raft in Blue
  Water